The Easter God

Also by John V. Taylor

The Primal Vision, 1963
The Go-Between God, 1972
Enough is Enough, 1974
A Matter of Life and Death, 1986
Weep Not For Me, 1986
Kingdom Come, 1989
The Christlike God, 1992

The
Easter God

and His Easter People

John V. Taylor

continuum
LONDON • NEW YORK

Continuum
The Tower Building, 11 York Road, London SE1 7NX
370 Lexington Avenue, New York, NY 10017–6503

British Library Cataloguing in Publication Data
A catalogue record for this is available
from the British Library

ISBN 0-8264-6630-3

Typeset by BookEns Ltd, Royston
Printed and bound in Great Britain by Biddles Ltd,
Guildford and King's Lynn

Contents

Foreword

When John Vernon Taylor died in January 2001, the newspaper obituaries were full of such phrases as: 'one of the most gifted and widely admired churchmen of his time'; 'one of the great missionaries of his generation'; 'prophet, artist, poet, musician'; 'an inspiring preacher who sought to persuade by the sheer reasonableness of his thinking'. Those who were privileged to know John realize that his greatest gift was to be able to inspire others with his assurance of the God of love who was for all people, and who could be experienced as much outside the church as within it.

After ordination and parish ministry, John felt called to work in Africa, and in 1945 was sent by the Church Missionary Society to be warden of Bishop Tucker College in Uganda, where he was responsible for training clergy, many of whom became the first African bishops. His unrivalled knowledge of Africa was to be of great service later to the Anglican Church, and his deep love for the country and its people remained with him throughout his life. It was his desire to 'search for the true meeting-place where Christ is conversing with the soul of Africa' that led him in 1963 to write *The Primal Vision*, 'immeasurably the most exciting piece of writing about Africa that I have yet come across from the pen of a white man', as one reviewer said, and a book 'which forces the critic to his knees'.

After a period as a research worker with the International Missionary Council, John become Africa Secretary for the Church Missionary Society and then, in 1963, its General Secretary. The CMS newsletters he produced each month were not only beautifully written, but demonstrated theology engaging with the world. During this time he wrote the book for which he is perhaps best known, *The Go-Between God*, which grew out of an earlier series of Edward Cadbury Lectures in

Theology, and which won the Collins Religious Book Award for the best religious book by a British author published in the period 1971–73. Almost coinciding with the announcement of his appointment to the bishopric of Winchester came *Enough is Enough*, a book which had grown out of the CMS newsletters and was way ahead of its time in its denouncement of our get-richer and have-more society.

When John Taylor was consecrated in Westminster Abbey on 31 January 1975, he became the first priest to be consecrated directly to the important see of Winchester since the Middle Ages. His stature, in the eyes of the church and the world, was already great. The Bishop of Winchester is the fifth senior bishop in the Church of England, and at that time had an automatic seat in the House of Lords. During the next ten years the diocese was infused with his intellectual and spiritual leadership, but it was his ability to communicate, and to get alongside people where they are, for which he will be best remembered. In 1979 he led a pilgrimage from Dorchester-on-Thames to Winchester, to celebrate the 900th anniversary of the move of the diocese to the city, walking and talking with his companion pilgrims of all ages along the way. He made sensitive use of radio and television to share the Gospel, and filled the cathedral with music and drama, which he loved. In 1981 he directed the opera *Passion and Resurrection* in the cathedral, using his artistic skills with great success to make the story real to others. His own 'Rosewindow' contributions to the monthly diocesan newsletters are theological works of art in miniature.

After his retirement in 1985, John lived in Oxford with his wife Peggy. They enjoyed some travelling, and had more time to devote to music and the theatre. John continued to write, for which he had had little time at Winchester, and was able to complete his other major work, *The Christlike God*, published in 1992. He wrote poetry, too, and went on speaking and preaching regularly until his last illness. His ability to communicate in poetic prose the reality of the God who is alive and makes us alive remained constant.

I met John in 1971 when, as his editor at SCM Press, I worked with him on *The Go-Between God*, and subsequently on all his other books published by the press. John was a hard taskmaster because he was an artist and a perfectionist. He would want to alter a word at the last minute, because it wasn't quite right – the sort of thing that usually drives editors to despair. But I worked gladly and humbly with John, because he was that kind of person.

After John died, Peggy asked me to look through his unpublished papers, many of which were sermons covering the period from his time at Winchester until a year or so before his death. It is sometimes said that all preachers only ever preach one sermon. I began to see one theme in particular – that of the God who brings love by loving through the darkness and into the light, through death and into life; who gives life by constantly stripping away what is past and urging us into the future, who dares us both to let go and to go beyond the ordinary. God's commitment to his people is shown in the life of his son, Jesus, whom he raised from death to life, and the outworking of his love is the Spirit which brings his people fully alive in his present kingdom. There are no certainties; we must live with uncertainties and risks, but the Christian hope is in this Easter God who has promised us that we shall have life, and have it abundantly.

The material on which I have drawn comes mainly but not exclusively from within a liturgical setting, and like all his writing is alive with the visual, musical and poetic imagery that was so much part of John. Inevitably it contains references linking to a particular time or context; I have edited it only very lightly to remove the most obvious of these, or those which were not necessary for the argument. John's sermons, like his books, were carefully crafted, and it is no one's place to tamper with them. They follow very roughly the cycle of the Christian year, from the Advent hope through the incarnation to the triumph of Easter and its fulfilment in the life-giving events of Pentecost. Those in the first part are centred on the nature of this God who raises us to life, those in the second on how he works in and through us to give life to the world. That this pattern can indeed be seen in preaching which spans a 25-year period is a tribute to John's spiritual integrity and the clarity of his vision.

'Recognition is the special gift of the Holy Spirit. It is the way he intervenes. He works always by opening people's eyes to see what they have not seen before.' It was John Taylor's special gift to open people's eyes to what they have not seen before.

Margaret Lydamore
August 2002

PART ONE

The God Who Gives Life

At a turn of the head bent intent on a task,
ripple of light, hem of his garment only,
or lift of the heart suddenly less lonely
is all the Easter evidence I ask.

1

In the End Is the Beginning

Sunday after Sunday Christians repeat in their creed: 'He will come again in glory to judge the living and the dead.' There was a time when that belief in another coming and a final judgement was one of the most essential features of the Christian faith. In the Middle Ages it was depicted in vivid realism on the west wall of many parish churches. It was the necessary context for all the other doctrines, all the festivals of Christianity. History is moving towards an end and a fulfilment which will also be a new beginning. The old will then be wound up and done away with to make room for the new, and that is why there will be a final reckoning and restitution so that nothing spoiled, nothing unresolved, will be left over to mar the new creation. That, they were sure of in those days. That was what lay ahead, and the whole story of redemption – Christ's incarnation and atonement and exaltation and the gift of the Holy Spirit – made sense only in the setting of that scenario of the end and the new beginning. That belief, 'he will come again', was present in the background of every Christmas, every Good Friday, every Easter and Whitsun, and every saint's day. It had no need of any special commemoration of its own. It was an ever-present fact. It wasn't any more in the minds of Christians on Advent Sunday than on any other day of the year. Advent was, and still is, primarily a run-up to Christmas, a sort of prelude, making us more ready to enter into the excitement and the realization and the wonder of the first coming of Christ.

Thomas Cranmer, who in 1549 produced the first English prayer book, the forerunner of the Book of Common Prayer, drew together the first and second comings of Christ and combined the shepherds' pipes of Bethlehem with the trumpets of Doomsday in the music of the beautiful collect for Advent Sunday:

Almighty God, give us grace to cast away the works of darkness and put on the armour of light, now in the time of this mortal life in which your Son Jesus Christ came to visit us in great humility, so that on the last day when he shall come again in his glorious majesty to judge the living and the dead, we may rise to the life immortal.

Perhaps he did that because he had a strong sense of the continuous rhythm of the Christian year, so that as we come to the end we are already at the beginning. On Advent Sunday, the first Sunday of the liturgical year, we both look back to Bethlehem and forward to the end. The first and the second coming overlap in people's eyes. In my end is my beginning – my beginning is my end.

Perhaps there is another reason. I believe that Cranmer, through his contacts with the other cities of Europe, was sensitive to the winds of rationalism, of renaissance, blowing through Europe and he knew that the image of the end would no longer be such a certainty. It would be far more difficult for people in the future to have that clear concept of history moving to an end, of a second coming, of a judgement – much harder to imagine.

Most of all, I think, Cranmer was aware that reformation itself was going to bring individualism of faith. It was no longer something that involved the world, no longer something that necessitated the future of humanity. It was much more *myself*, *my* faith, *my* relationship to God through Jesus Christ. I am going to heaven, rather than he is coming again to earth. And isn't that where we actually stand? What does his coming again to this earth mean to us? In what sense is this necessary when our minds are fixed on making ourselves ready to go to him in heaven? Isn't it a going rather than a coming that ends our very individualistic concept of God's purpose? I believe that we have lost the sense of God's love for the world and the relationships of the world, and we are satisfied with a vague sense of spiritual unity, floating around, disembodied, without relationship, just somehow swallowed up in God.

Advent is the time of the Advent antiphons, a version of which we still sing in the hymn 'O come, O come, Emmanuel!' And those Advent antiphons aren't just the first scene of a nativity play re-enacting the coming at Bethlehem. We are not just making ourselves better ready to remember that past coming, we are actually crying out for something new, something that will resolve the conflicts. Nations matter, so that it means something to look forward to a time when nation will not raise up sword against nation, but all the nations will bring their glory into the city. Is that all meaningless, must we leave all that, or somehow make it a vague interpretation of a vague existence in the future, all with God?

No, there is a cry, and it is necessarily in Jewish terms, as we take up the antiphons of Advent. They are all harking back to an Old Testament hope that God will eventually bring a resolution, a culmination. For his purpose in this world creation does matter. I have to confess, though, that I cannot imagine, I no longer have a picture at the back of my mind of that final ending, of a new beginning. I can't imagine it. I only know that deep in my heart there is a sense of an ending, of a resolution. My love of music tells me so. A tune doesn't just suddenly stop, hanging in the air. Somehow even in the most modern music it comes to a resolution, there is a kind of sense of the end, that makes sense of it all. And don't we have just that cry in our hearts, 'Lord, how long?' And in that cry we are saying there will be an ending, all the promises of God will be fulfilled, and they will be fulfilled in Jesus Christ. In him is the 'Yes' to all God's promises. I don't know how; I wish I did. But I do think that I can say with the poet Edwin Muir:

> But he will come again, it's said, though not
> Unwanted and unsummoned; for all things,
> Beasts of the field, and woods, and rocks, and seas,
> And all mankind from end to end of the earth
> Will call him with one voice. In our own time,
> Some say, or at a time when time is ripe.
> Then he will come, Christ the uncrucified,
> Christ the discrucified, his death undone,
> His agony unmade, his cross dismantled –
> Glad to be so – and the tormented wood
> Will cure its hurt and grow into a tree
> In a green springing corner of young Eden.
> And Judas damned take his long journey backward
> From darkness into light and be a child
> Beside his mother's knee, and the betrayal
> Be quite undone and never more be done.[1]

---

[1] Edwin Muir, 'The Transfiguration', *Collected Poems*, Faber 1963, p. 198.

Yes, that hope lies in our hearts, that hope is promised us, though we can't imagine it. This world makes sense, this world is loved by God and matters to God, and in some way – unimaginable – this world will achieve its total fulfilment in Jesus Christ.

2

In the Beginning Was the Word

In the beginning was the Word, and the Word was with God,
and the Word was God. (John 1.1)

'In the beginning was the Word.' Which word? I know that sounds like a stupid question, an ignorant question, because this opening verse of John's Gospel isn't talking about human speech or the sort of words we use. It's talking about God's self-expression, God's revelation of himself. All the same, the writer of this passage has chosen to use this metaphor, this picture of God in the beginning, so perhaps he did mean us to look at it more closely, and even to ask that stupid question. Let me phrase it a little differently.

If you can think of God at a time when nothing had yet been created, a time when there is no time, no space, nothing at all except the limitless energy of love which we call God, what do you imagine God is thinking? What is he saying? He's thinking of love and the infinite purposes and promises of love. There is nothing else to be thought. And what is his response to those thoughts, those purposes and promises of love? What word do you feel he would say? 'Yes, O yes!' The 'Yes' of delight and recognition, 'That's right', which an artist or a scientist shouts inwardly when she or he hits on the perfect solution. The 'Yes' of one who volunteers to carry out a superb plan when it has been made clear. Yes! So be it! Amen!

Of course this is all imagining, all picture-language. But since our human minds are incapable of grasping anything that might be called literally true about God, picture-language is all we've got. And the opening of John's Gospel encourages us to think along the lines I have suggested.

In the beginning was the Word, whatever word it was, and the Word was 'with' God. The Greek that the author uses at this point is remarkable. It actually means 'and the Word was towards God and the Word was God'. It is God's response to God's own being. We find the same form of words used in a bad sense in Luke's Gospel in the parable of the Pharisee and the publican, where Jesus says the Pharisee was 'standing towards himself' and that he prayed 'towards himself'. In fact that is what was wrong with his prayer. In his letter to the Romans Paul says that when we are right with God we have peace with God, and he uses the same word: peace towards God, peace in relation to God. So the Word which was in the beginning is a Word directed towards God. It is an exclamation of response called forth by God. It is a cry of welcome and dedication to all that is purposed and promised by the eternal energy of divine love. And it is God who speaks that Word. The Word was God, God's own 'Yes' to God's own loving will.

As I've said, it is all a metaphor, a picture. And you can see how it matches that other picture-metaphor of Christian talk which speaks of God's eternal will to love as the Father because it is the source of all else, and speaks of God's responding 'Yes' to that will as God-the-Son because it is called forth and begotten by that will and purpose.

Other New Testament writers also put the two metaphor-pictures together, in order to say that God the Son is simply God the Word, the responding Word of delight and dedication, God's 'O yes!' to the unchanging purpose and promise of God's will to love. In the first chapter of his second letter to the church in Corinth Paul says:

> The Son of God, Jesus Christ, whom we preached among you was not a blend of Yes and No. In him it is always 'Yes'. For he is the Yes, the Amen, pronounced upon God's promises, every one of them. That's why, when we give glory to God it is in him, Jesus Christ, that *we* say Amen, Yes.

So the Word, God's joyous, sacrificial 'Yes' to God's purpose of love, became a human being like one of us, and every action, every thought, every prayer of that man Jesus of Nazareth, every breath of his living and dying, repeated that eternal 'Yes'. 'The Word became flesh and dwelt among us; we saw his glory, such glory as befits God's only Son, full of grace and truth.'

God's 'Yes'. God the Son. The first-begotten, original 'Yes'. But not the one and only Son. For to all who did receive him amid so many who have not, to those who have yielded him their allegiance, he gave the right to become God's children, brothers and sisters of

God the Son, human echoes of God's own 'Yes' to love's eternal plan.

What will it cost us to exercise our right to become members of that family? To answer that question, here is a true story. A friend who was a devoted Quaker used often to attend summer holiday camps for families in the USA. One afternoon he went down to a lake with a number of children with the intention of swimming, and then suddenly thought it would be nice to take a boat out on the lake. He didn't discover until he got to the quay where the boats were moored that he was allowed to take only five on board, including one adult. He had with him six children and knew that two of them would have to be disappointed. He looked at them and wondered – and his eyes fell on a brother and sister with whom he was particularly close. The girl was 11 and the boy was only 9. They were as eager as the others to go on the trip. He knew that he loved them more than the others, and he guessed they were aware of it. He deliberately said to them, 'I'm sorry, I won't be able to take you.' They made no complaint and, afterwards, their mother said to him, 'You don't know how proud they were that you had treated them like members of your own family, and trusted them to understand why you chose them for the hard part of letting the others go in the boat.'

To be given the right to become children of God is to be trusted to echo God's own delighted, 'Yes, O yes!' to the way of self-giving love, and to each difficult step of that way as we come to it.

3

The Moment in Time

The Christian year begins on Advent Sunday. That is both the end and the beginning. To think of Advent properly we have to imagine that we are at the end of time, which is also the beginning of timelessness. The Christian year goes round and round, and where it ends, there it begins. It is a circle, representing eternity, for our faith speaks of eternal things, beyond the straight line of history.

But the calendar year goes on and on in the long straight line of evolving history. It is a good thing, when history seems too much for us, to remember that it is all taking place within the vast circle and stillness of eternity. There is something besides the on and on, one damned thing after another. There is a meaning and there is a love pervading and watching over all. And yet time does matter to God. God isn't above it. And that is the message of Christmas, of the incarnation. God hasn't stayed in his eternity, outside one damned thing after another, outside our troubled history of black and white, good and bad, our ambiguous time. God came down to earth, down into history, in order to assure us that he takes our time seriously and he is with us in it all,

Many, many streams of cause and effect, going back into an infinite past, converged upon the baby that was born to Mary, just as so many causes and effects converged on you and me, making us what we are. God did not become incarnate in a human vacuum. He became part of the process, subject to the process, a victim of it, if you like, a child of his age. And Jesus Christ wove his life together out of the material that he was given, just as you and I have to do. That is why the Gospels stress the fact that it was when the Emperor Augustus was on the throne, and Quirinius was the Governor of Syria, it was an actual moment in history when this particular child was born in a particular place and took on exactly the same burden of humanity as all of us have to carry.

God is not beyond and above it all; he is right within it all. He has always been within it all, within the enormous processes of evolution, within the development of your life from your childhood up to today, and he will be involved in your life to the very end and long beyond that. God has involved himself in the changes and chances of time. And that is why we may never look back and think, 'Oh, if only': if only I'd had a better deal; if only I'd had more chances; if only I'd made more of my chances; if only I hadn't made so many mistakes. That is to regard God, and indeed your own fate, as something beyond the here and now, but it isn't.

If God is to be of any use to you or me, he has to be a God who stands gently alongside you, and says, 'Where shall we go from here? What shall we make of it?' You can't undo what has made you what you are. You can't undo history. But from this moment, with God you can look forward and say, 'What shall we make of this?' Looking forward may cause many of us a certain frisson of fear. What will this year bring upon the world? Will it only add to the meaninglessness of everything? Shall we be able to cope with whatever comes? It is when we are worried in those terms that it is good to remember that the child born at Bethlehem reminds us that God says, 'Let's take it from here, and whatever comes, let's see what we can make of it.'

Now anyone may object that New Year's Eve and New Year's Day are not church celebrations. Most people think that New Year's Eve is the time for the revellers in Piccadilly Circus. And perhaps we look down our noses a little bit and think maybe we oughtn't to be celebrating this evening. But Christmas, after all, should remind us that God is the God who has come into the life of the world – God in the ordinary, in the secular. George MacLeod, the great Scottish prophet who founded the Iona Community, never ceased to enjoy telling the story of the Christmas decorations over one small town which he happened to visit in South Africa, where the final E had come adrift so that the banner read, GLORY TO GOD IN THE HIGH ST! And we need to see God's glory in the high street and the supermarkets at this time.

It is interesting, though, that the secular world never quite kept a certain date for the beginning of its new year. It wasn't always 1 January. The Normans, in fact, introduced Lady Day, 25 March, I suppose, as the beginning of the whole Christmas story with the annunciation to the Virgin Mary. At any rate, from the time of the Normans right up until 1752, New Year's Day was 25 March. I am not quite sure how they changed it in 1752, whether they made an extraordinarily long year or cut one short, but in that year they went back to the ancient Roman custom of starting the year on 1 January, which of course is how it was in the time of Jesus. *Janua* means a door, a house-door, from which we get our name janitor, the doorkeeper, and there was a god who was the doorkeeper, called Janus, who had two heads, two faces, one looking back and one looking forward. But his real name meant the sunrise, because even then people looked forward to a new year with hope. Maybe it will be more like bright daylight than the last one was.

I think Jesus identifies with this undying human hope. Perhaps we can do better next time. And Jesus comes quietly alongside every human being who has that hope, and says, 'Yes, you can.' And that is what makes him the door. He is not only the door for Christians, he is the door for every human being who looks forward with a bit of hope and wants to move through into something new. Jesus says, 'Yes, if anyone moves through into the new through me, he will be safe.'

New Year is always a milestone, another mark on time's clock. There are two ways of looking at time; again it is the secular or the sacred. Secular time, again in the old world, was called *chronos*. One of the most ancient gods of all, the grandfather of Zeus, was called Chronos, from which, of course, we get our word chronometer. Our watches, our clocks are the measures of *chronos*. Shakespeare talked about the *chronicle* of wasted time. All that time past, and we still haven't arrived. Year after year, month after month, minute after minute, time moves on and sometimes we despair of it. Tomorrow and tomorrow and tomorrow ... But is it all vanity, useless? It can bring us to despair if we think of time as *chronos*. That is why Jesus said to his disciples just before he left them in this world at the time of his ascension, 'It is not for you to know the times or seasons, or to worry about them', and he used that word *chronos*. Take no thought for tomorrow and tomorrow and tomorrow, because that is not the time-scale in which you have to live.

The other word is God's time, the word is *kairos*, the hour. 'My hour', says Jesus, 'is not yet come.' What did he mean? They all looked at their watches – surely it is six o'clock, isn't it? Yes, but he had his time. And we have ours; you have yours, I have mine. Some day, some time, an hour strikes, and we can say, 'Father, the hour has come.' This is it. Something now is going to change. Something now is going to happen. It is the hour, one crowded hour of glorious life, and moments like that happen to any one of us. Sometimes terrible moments of decision, moments of tragedy, from which something can be made. It may be the last moment, when finally we go through the last door into life to come. And who knows for which of us that may happen in these coming twelve months? But what does *chronos* matter if we enter the *kairos*, the moment, with Jesus, because we have been holding his hand all along the way.

So let us resolve to go into the coming year with Jesus at this moment, staying close to him all along the road, and in that way we shall be ready for the hour that really matters, those hours whenever God happens to send them to us. They will be our hour and his hour if we are with him, and we shall be safe.

4

The Shining Appearance

Evangelism, preaching the gospel, is at the heart of Christianity. But what ought we to be doing? Do we really believe in evangelism? It is valuable, in fact necessary, to remember that evangelism is only the third stage in a process in which the chief actor is God. For the whole process consists of preparation, manifestation, communication. Preparation, manifestation – and then, and only then – communication, which is what we mean by evangelism.

Just consider God's preparation for the Gospel. God was at work long before you were dreamed of, preparing the new ingredients of your life. For example, consider our celebration of Christmas. The winter solstice takes place year by year, when our planet reaches the furthest point away from the sun, and appears to pause there in that remote point before starting to draw near to the sun again. And through all the ages men have been aware of that moment of extremest cold and darkness. Two thousand years before Christ, in Alexandria, the Egyptians drew up a new calendar, and placed the observance of that winter solstice on 6 January, or rather, putting it the right way round, they arranged the calendar so that 6 January coincided with that furthest point away from the sun, the winter solstice. Because they were aware of that, they called that day the birthday of the god Osiris, the god of life – furthest away, now at last born in the darkness, life returning.

And that went on and on, century after century, until by the year 400 BC, because of a certain inaccuracy in their calendar – similar to the one in ours which has to be corrected with a leap year – the winter solstice was now occurring on 25 December. Again they called that the birthday of a god, the god Mithras, the Persian god of light. Mithras was particularly popular among the soldiers of the Roman armies, and therefore his cult spread all over the world, even up here in Britain. And at the same time, roughly, and for the same sort of reason, the Jewish people celebrated the restoration of worship in the desecrated Temple after the victories of the nationalistic movement of the Maccabees with the festival which they still keep round about 20 or 22 December because of the winter solstice, the feast they call Hannukah, or 'the feast of lights'.

So the great festivals of the ending of darkness and the returning of light on 25 December and on 6 January were established as the birthdays of a god. And very naturally the Eastern Christians chose 6 January, the day they established in the Alexander calendar, for the birthday and the baptism of Jesus, calling it, as they do today, not Epiphany but Theophany – the appearance of God. At the same time the Western Christians, because of the greater influence of that worship of the Roman army, favoured 25 December since that was the greater of the two pagan festivals in Italy. But later they wanted to observe 6 January as well and so in the West it was turned into the festival for remembering the coming of the Wise Men.

That little bit of history reminds us that long, long before there were any Christians or any good news to be proclaimed, God was patiently preparing the symbols which would convey the meaning, and was preparing the people for whom these symbols would be so significant, as they are still for us today. God knew what he was going to do. He quietly prepared people and the world itself for that great event, and it is still true that God goes before us preparing the way, before there can be any thought of evangelism.

Then comes, once again, God's action, his manifestation, his epiphany. The word means both an appearing and a shining – a shining appearance. What was so long a secret in God's mind, and was so long in preparation before the fullness of time had come, is now at last made visible, it is shown and people can see it with their eyes. So in the second letter to Timothy, Paul writes of 'God's gracious purpose, which was granted to us in Christ Jesus from all eternity, but has now at last been brought fully into view by the appearance of our saviour Jesus Christ'. 'Fully into view' – a baby in a manger.

But that same word of epiphany, or revealing or appearance, applied not only to the incarnation but also to that future day to which the world looks forward when in the letter to Titus Paul says, 'For the grace of God bringing salvation has appeared to all people' – that is, on Christmas Day – 'teaching us to live so truly and for God in this present world, while we look for that blessed hope and the glorious appearing' – the same word, epiphany – 'of the great God and our saviour Jesus Christ.' There is to be a future epiphany to which we look and which must be part of our evangelism. It is a shining appearance always, so in the second letter to the Thessalonians, Paul speaks of 'the radiance of his coming', the epiphany, the same word, 'the radiance of his coming'. And it comes again in the Benedictus, the song of Zechariah from the first chapter of Luke's Gospel, which says that he is to appear visibly, to give light to them that sit in darkness and in the shadow of death. Epiphany – a radiant appearing of God in our midst, a theophany. And so in the Greek translation of the Old Testament it is applied to the pillar of fire that shone, leading the people of Israel forward as the story is told in the book of Exodus, the symbol of the presence of God in their midst, something they could see and know that God was real and with them, God's gift, God's coming to us.

God is constantly giving himself to us in visible form. It is in visible form that he gives himself to us in the sacrament of the eucharist. And always these are his epiphanies, his shining appearance of his own reality.

It is that gift of his appearing to us, so that we know and we have seen, that is the basis of our evangelism. There is no evangelism except in response to his appearing, his self-giving. Consider the shepherds on Christmas Day, keeping watch by night. There was something quite mundane, quite normal; it had gone on year after year; it was their patient duty, and through it God was preparing them for the moment of their epiphany, when the glory of the Lord shone round about them and they saw the bright light and they heard the voice, 'I bring you good news' – that is the word evangelism – 'I evangelize you about a great joy, a saviour is born to you', a personal appearance concerning a personal knowledge of God, a nearness of God that was for them. And after that, and only after that, comes their obedient response: 'Let us go and see', put the news to the test, make sure of it for ourselves. 'And when they saw the babe in the manger they made known what had been told them', so that others heard and were surprised. They couldn't keep it to themselves, for they had seen with their own eyes. What had been real to them was naturally passed on to others. There was their evangelism.

We see exactly the same pattern in the Wise Men. They saw the rising of a star, they were pursuing their craft as astrologers, people who had to foretell, forecast, what was likely to happen. 'We have seen his star.' And that was their evangel, that was their response. They didn't remain satisfied that a king had been born, they must go and see for themselves, they must pay homage. And so in those brief words there is summed up that long journey, all the care with which they prepared for it, all the hardships of the way until at last they came to Jerusalem, and still were questioning. Remember, our evangelism, if it is to ring true, will also contain our questioning – where is he? – because we know he is around, we have seen the arising of a star. They conveyed their message, responding.

And their message was very disturbing. It is good news of great joy, but it is also good news of a great disturbance. So we must not be afraid when people react in different ways when we share what to us is such good news. For some it will be deeply disturbing, and that is a sign of the life-giving power of the revelation. Herod was greatly disturbed, and the whole of Jerusalem with him, and evangelism may well disturb the peace and threaten the status quo. It is all summed up for us in the very first verse of the first letter of John, and I believe we should take this verse as a guide to any true evangelism. 'It was there from the beginning', God at work, silently preparing. It is something eternal we are dealing with in our evangelism; we don't have to think it up, it isn't a new gimmick. 'It was there from the beginning.' And then the revelation, the epiphany, 'We have heard it, we have seen it with our own eyes, we looked upon it, and felt it with our own hands, and it is this that we tell'– there comes the evangelism. 'Our theme is the Word of life.'

5

From Revelation to Revolution

It is interesting to compare the various Sunday lectionaries in the different service books. Those who drew up these courses of readings, especially in their choice of the Gospels, evidently held different views as to what the season of Epiphany is actually about. The Roman Catholic Church doesn't really observe an Epiphanytide at all beyond the remainder of the week after Epiphany, and within this week the Gospel readings focus on different demonstrations of Christ's miraculous power. The Alternative Service Book does designate the succeeding Sundays as Sundays after Epiphany, but its choice of Gospels wavers between the Roman Missal and a rather uncomprehending imitation of the Book of Common Prayer. So every January, I find myself preferring, as an indication of theme at this stage in the church's year, the series of Gospel readings given in the Book of Common Prayer for Epiphany and the succeeding Sundays. For Ephipany itself we have the story of Herod, and on the following five Sundays the stories of Jesus in the Temple, of the marriage at Cana, of the centurion's servant, of the stilling of the storm and the Gadarene swine, and finally of the wheat and the tares.

In Luke's Gospel the first effect of the coming of Christ into the world was to startle a few shepherds out in the fields. In Matthew's Gospel the first consequence of the birth of Christ was the agitation of a whole city. 'Herod the King was greatly perturbed when he heard this and all Jerusalem with him.' Luke gives us a pastoral scene of flocks and pastures, the village inn and a manger for the beasts. Matthew takes us to the streets of the capital and the intrigues of the palace. The one story tells of a heavenly declaration of peace, the other tells of a very down-to-earth disturbance of the peace. And that is the theme of the whole of Epiphanytide.

The kingship of Jesus is not of this world, yet it challenges every

worldly throne and every institution of human power and organiza-
tion. When Herod heard of a star that signified the birth of a new
king, he had reason to be troubled, for the great disturber of the city
had come. On a later occasion when Jesus came to Jerusalem as an
adult, Matthew's Gospel tells us 'all the city was shaken, and asked,
"Who is this?"' And after Jesus' resurrection, when his story began to
spread out over the Roman empire, we read that in Iconium 'the mass
of the townspeople were divided'; in Philippi they complained to the
magistrates that 'these men are causing a disturbance in our city'; in
Ephesus 'the whole city was in confusion and uproar'; and the citizens
of Thessalonika exclaimed: 'The men who have turned the world
upside down have come here also.' So it was to be expected that when
a working party of Christian thinkers produced a report called *Faith in
the City*, one member of parliament at least would brand it as Marxist
philosophy. The Wise Men came to Bethlehem straight from the
corridors of power, where a diplomatic understanding had been
reached, but after their encounter with Mary's child they would no
longer play Herod's game. A tiny beginning of a universal revolt had
taken place.

'Do not think that I came to bring peace on earth', says Jesus. 'I
came not to send peace, but a sword.'

This theme of disturbance is renewed in the Gospel for the first
Sunday after Epiphany, though now it occurs in the domestic context
of the family. The wonderfully reassuring incident of the boy Jesus in
the Temple, as told in the second chapter of Luke's Gospel, is the
story of any pre-adolescent child kicking over the traces, not being
conveniently where his parents expected him to be and consequently
throwing them into hours, possibly days, of acute anxiety. He had
gone his own way without telling them, and they were taken aback
and confused like the parents of any other teenager. We can recognize
that frightened sharpening of the voice in Mary's reproach: 'Son, why
have you done this to us? Your father and I have been terribly
worried, searching for you.' And he, with the devastating directness of
the young: 'Why were you searching for me? Didn't you know I must
be on my Father's business now?' I don't think he was claiming any
precocious religious vocation. 'Being about his Father's business' was
his way of saying what every adolescent boy or girl is bound to say – 'I
must stop being what you, my parents, want me to be. I must grow up
to be what I am meant to be. That is my Father's business.' That claim
must be stated, that small personal revolt must take place, even in the

most loving family, and the pain of that disturbance is the price of the glorious freedom of the children of God.

The second Sunday carries us on to the wedding party at Cana, five miles from Nazareth, at the home of some relative or friend of the family. The significance of this turning of water into wine is often missed. The other evangelists all emphasize that at the start of his ministry Jesus had a lot to say about the new wine of the life of the kingdom of God. It couldn't be contained in the old bottles. The second chapter of John's Gospel shows him demonstrating that teaching in a sign, an acted parable. Before dealing with the shortage of wine at the feast Jesus orders the servants to fill to the brim the six great stone jars that held the water for that family's ritual washings of hands and head and utensils. Those jars symbolized the religious observance of the law and Jesus had not come to destroy this but to fulfil it. But when that was done he sent the servants back to the well itself. The words 'draw out' mean to draw water from the well, as we see in the encounter with the woman of Samaria, two chapters further on. So in this almost silent drama Jesus is saying, 'Don't reject the law and its rituals. But don't merely repeat what has been handed on from the past. Go back to the God from whom your fathers drew their inner life and find in him direct the new wine for a new day.'

That message was a profound disturbance to the guardians of the water jars, the custodians of the tradition. It still is. And so was the incident recalled in the third Sunday's reading when Jesus extended the freedom of his Father's kingdom to a Gentile centurion, unconverted and uncircumcised. As if to ram home the shocking enormity of this inclusiveness, Matthew tells as a prelude the story of the healing of the leper. The strict believer was expected to treat every Gentile as a contamination. But Jesus welcomed both leper and Roman, and in his disturbing honesty went so far as to prophesy that Gentiles would pour into the kingdom of God from every quarter of the globe before the true children of the Covenant were ready to enter.

The reading for the fourth Sunday, from the eighth chapter of Matthew's Gospel, shows the Lord calming the storm of demon possession with the same quiet authority that he exercised over the storm of wind and rain on the lake. And yet this glorious liberation was seen by the people of that region as only another unwelcome disturbance of their peace – and they begged him to go away.

By the time you have completed the Sundays after Epiphany there is no doubt where the journey through Lent is going to end.

The manifestation of Jesus Christ to the world spreads outwards in ever widening circles. Its light falls afresh into our own lives as year on year goes by. But there can be no true revelation which is not also revolution. That is the message of Epiphany.

> I saw a stable, low and very bare,
> A little child in a manger.
> The oxen knew him, had him in their care,
> To men he was a stranger.
> The safety of the world was lying there
> And the world's danger.[1]

[1] Mary Elizabeth Coleridge (1861–1907).

6

The Wine Poured Forth

Lord, you should know that your friend is ill. (John 11.3)

The fifth Sunday in Lent has for centuries been called Passion Sunday, though Roman Catholics have recently taken to transferring that title to the next Sunday. So at first sight it seems a bit inappropriate to read of the raising of Lazarus on the Sunday when we think of the beginning of our Lord's Passion. But when we read the story carefully we can see that that is exactly what John's Gospel makes of it. The Passion of Jesus, its inevitability, began when he decided to go back into Judaea and restore his friend Lazarus to life. More than that, the Gospel of John, which omits the agony in the garden, gives us this story instead: Bethany is its Gethsemane.

Just consider how the story is told. The supreme Jewish authority under the Romans was the High Priest and his family and the officials who controlled the Temple. They were far more dangerous than the rabbis of the Pharisee party, and Jesus had incurred their hatred. They had not yet made up their minds to get rid of him, though an attempt had been made to arrest him which he had narrowly eluded. Now he had withdrawn beyond their reach into a neighbouring province on the far side of the River Jordan and his friends everywhere heaved a sigh of relief.

Among the most intimate of those friends were the sisters Martha and Mary and their brother Lazarus, who had moved from their native village and were now living at Bethany, a small suburb about two miles east of Jerusalem. Lazarus fell gravely ill. As he grew steadily worse the sisters must often have murmured, 'If only Jesus were here.' They wouldn't have wanted to bring him back into danger, but how they wished things had been different! They agreed eventually that at least they should let him know. After all, there were other people he had healed without going in person to their homes. So they sent their message: 'Lord, you should know that your friend is ill.' In fact, they had left it too late.

Jesus was at least a day's journey away, and according to the times given by the evangelist, when the message was delivered Lazarus was already dead. And by means of his extraordinary empathy with other people Jesus knew this, either immediately he heard of the sickness, or sometime afterwards. Yet his first response to the message was supremely positive and life-affirming: 'This sickness is not unto death but for the sake of the glory of God, that by its means the Son of God may be glorified.' Those words have been terribly misunderstood. They do not mean that God sends a fatal illness and plunges a family into desolation so that a miracle may bring honour to himself and to Jesus Christ. To glorify means to let the true nature shine out, the inner nature coming outside so that it can be seen. And self-aggrandizement at the expense of others is not the true nature of God or of Jesus. Jesus, in fact, never asked what caused a misfortune or why it was sent. For him the only question that mattered was, 'What shall we make of this? What purpose can it be made to serve?' On this occasion what his words mean is: 'This sickness shall not serve death's purpose but it shall be the means whereby the true nature of God, and of his Servant-Son, will shine out.' But what Jesus understood by the true nature of God, and how it was to shine out, remained to be seen.

He had made his decision without hesitation: the outcome was to be a victory for life, not death. He had made it out of love, for it is at this point, immediately after that declaration of intent, that the Gospel inserts the statement: 'Now Jesus loved Martha and her sister and Lazarus.' Because of love the outcome was going to be life, not death. Yet he waited two days. Knowing intuitively that his friend had died there was no need to rush back; but having resolved what to make of the tragedy, why did Jesus hold back? What was he doing during those two days? His next words to the disciples give us the clue: 'Let us go into Judaea again.' It was Judaea that had been in his mind during that mysterious hesitation – not Bethany, not Lazarus. It was going to be life for them. But the price of that life – Judaea. The disciples knew at once what that name meant. 'Master, it was only just now that the Jews tried to stone you. Are you going there again?' Jesus answered, 'There are only twelve hours of daylight, aren't there? The time for travelling is then, when you can see the road. If you leave it too late when it's dark again, you'll stumble.' Had Jesus, I wonder, experienced that night, that loss of direction during the two days while he wrestled with the implications of his love and of that decision, and was he determined to seize a new moment of clarity and make the fatal journey without further stumbling in the dark?

So then Jesus explained what it was that had prompted his decision, first in metaphor: 'Our friend Lazarus has fallen asleep but I am going to wake him', and then with brutal directness: 'Lazarus died.' And at that the thought returns to Jesus, 'What do we make of this?' and with it a renewal of joy: 'I am glad for your sakes that I was not there to prevent this death, for it will bring about your belief.' Belief in what? Your belief. Your trust in the true nature of God.

So, on the third day after receiving the message from Bethany they made the arduous journey back and were seen approaching the outskirts of the village by some of the friends who had come out from Jerusalem to condole with the two bereaved sisters. They passed the word to Martha, who hurried out to meet Jesus and the disciples on the road, and there she learned the secret of his idea of time. The only time which meant anything to him was not the past ('If only you had been here'), nor the future ('I know he will rise again on the last day'), but the present ('I am the resurrection and the life'). Life is always and only now. And now the true life of all things was going to give itself to Lazarus out of love.

But how does life give itself? By means of that mysterious law of the universe which Charles Williams called the doctrine of exchange. We can, and do, bear one another's burdens. One can lift away another person's fear or anxiety by undertaking to become worried or terrified instead of that person. We have almost lost the use of such powers, but they exist, and I think that most mothers are aware of them, and some lovers too. The capacity exists because it is the Creator's own reflection within his creation. Yes: life, God's life, lives by giving itself away out of love. It gives life to the dead by undergoing their death. That is the true nature of God, and Jesus knew that the hour had come for that sacrificial nature to shine out. By coming to give life to Lazarus, and not only to Lazarus but to God's whole beloved humanity, he had handed himself over to his destroyers. His life was to be given away so that Lazarus might come out of the tomb.

It was the other sister, Mary, who witnessed and, to some degree, shared his Gethsemane. She in her turn comes running and throws herself at his feet sobbing, 'If only you had been here', and her anguish seems to trigger off his own. The language which John's Gospel uses has baffled most commentators and translators, for it describes not the confident approach to an act of triumphant power, but a terrible inner conflict. It says he was swept by indignation as if in confronting some adversary. He was in shuddering distress; he shed tears and was visibly troubled. The portrayal is reminiscent of Mark's description of the agony in the garden: 'Horror and anguish overwhelmed him, and he said to them, my heart is ready to break with grief.' Then, as in Gethsemane, he went forward: 'Take away the stone.' And then the great cry: 'Lazarus, come out.' Then the final practical command: 'Loose him, and *let him go*' – the very phrase he was to use in Gethsemane again: 'If I am the man you want, *let these men go*.' Let him go. Let you and me go – into life.

As if to underline the price that Jesus paid for restoring life to Lazarus and hope to that family and life to the whole of mankind, John's Gospel rounds off the story with the words: 'Some of them went off to the Pharisees and reported what he had done. Thereupon the chief priests with the Pharisees convened a meeting of the Council. One of them, Caiaphas, who was High Priest that year said: It is more to your interest that one man should die on behalf of the people than that the whole nation should be destroyed.'

You and I do not have the power to raise the dead; we have not such supreme aliveness in us for that. Yet Jesus calls us, especially at Passiontide, to obey the inner law of life – all life. The law that life exists by giving itself away. Whoever seeks to keep life will lose it: whoever loses life for my sake will keep it for ever. In a poem called 'Sermon in a Hospital', written by the early nineteenth-century Italian poet Hugo Bassi, come the often-quoted words:

> Measure thy life by loss and not by gain;
> Not by the wine drunk, but the wine poured forth;
> For love's strength standeth in love's sacrifice;
> And who so suffers most hath most to give.

7

God Was in Christ

Religions are not invented by theologians, neither is faith the product of a drafting committee. Religions grow out of experiences, just like all other kinds of human knowledge. Religions are the fruit of experience and they come into being in order to reflect upon the experience, to interpret it and to conserve and pass on to subsequent generations the impact, the insights and effects of the original experience.

The experience may have been a numinous encounter with the mysterious otherness of a tree or a creature of the wild, the sudden unveiling of the splendour or menace of the world, the powerful impact of music or a great building, or the extraordinary significance of an ordinary occurrence. Such encounters, brooded over by those who experienced them, have generated the belief in an all-pervasive holy power which is the basis of primal religion. The originating experiences may have been brief moments of a mystical recognition of the essential oneness of all that is, the sense of its meaning, which has given rise to the perennial philosophy of much Asian religion. Other faiths, notably Judaism, have grown by continual reflection upon, and re-enactment of, an initial experience of total powerlessness or exceptional deliverance, a salvation or rescue of one sort or another, and this is also often the germ of an individual's faith. Or again, the impact of another human being, the life and personality rather than the teaching, is enough to revolutionize the values, hopes and actions of others. This is the case with devotees of some Hindu gurus and, most notably, it is this type of experience that gave birth to Christianity and goes on producing Christians still.

A parish priest who lives near us in Oxford has told me that during his first term at Cambridge a conversation with fellow students one evening touched on the subject of Jesus Christ. Although religion

had played no part in his life he was intrigued enough to borrow a
Bible and take it back to his rooms. He started on the Gospel of
Matthew and could not put it down, so captivated was he by the
figure of Jesus that emerged. He finished it in the small hours,
knowing that he had become a disciple. Before the end of the term he
was thinking seriously about ordination. Three years later he found
himself at a theological college where, ironically, his tutors seemed to
be unanimous in asserting that it is impossible to know anything with
certainty about the real Jesus.

Now of course it's true that the Gospels don't provide a biography
or literary portrait in the modern style; that was not their purpose.
These stories and sayings all reflected the beliefs which the Christians
who preserved them wanted to stress and the opposing views they
wanted to refute. Nevertheless, the Gospels do consistently reveal in
the Jesus they present certain incidental idiosyncrasies of style and
speech, an attitude towards people and a relationship with God from
all of which emerges a recognizable personality. There is, for example,
the daringly intimate term *Abba* with which Jesus addressed God, a
hallmark which, Paul claimed, Christians were entitled to adopt in
their own prayers. There is the other almost untranslatable aramaic
word, often re-iterated, *Amin amin*, 'Yes, yes' or 'Indeed, indeed',
with which Jesus liked to underline what he was about to say, and to
which Paul again refers: 'With him it is always "Yes".' A more careful
study of the parables, so-called, reveals a distinctive teaching method
which relies, not on stories with a double meaning, but on an appeal
to some everyday experience, sometimes comically exaggerated by
Jesus, with which his hearers can identify: 'Which of you, if you
owned a hundred sheep and found one was missing ...?' 'Which of
you, having an ox or an ass that fell down a well on Sunday ...?'
'Which of you, embarrassed by a friend's arrival in the middle of the
night, wouldn't knock up a neighbour ...?' It was a method that
invited people to give their own verdict, thereby pronouncing a
verdict on their own opinions; and it tells us a great deal about the
man who preferred it to other ways of teaching.

Those men and women who made up the first nucleus of the
Christian movement had experienced their encounter with Jesus as a
freelance rabbi who came from Nazareth. He appears to have been a
blood-relation to several of them. Within a few years of his death they
appointed James, the senior member of his family, to be the leader of
their community in Jerusalem and, on James's death, nearly 30 years

later, a younger cousin was chosen by the Judaean Christians to succeed him. So they could hardly fail to remember Jesus as a man who was one of themselves. He, like them, was a Jew by race and religion. He had inherited the history and the expectant hopes of that oppressed nation. As they saw more of him during the Galilean ministry they recognized that he had an intensely intimate relationship with God. They saw that he had exceptional powers. But he was not the only Jewish healer and exorcist, and according to the Gospel of Luke, even when he raised a widow's son from death, all that the bystanders said was, 'A great prophet has arisen among us', presumably remembering Elisha who had once done the same at nearby Shunem. Whatever Jesus did and whatever Jesus was, those who encountered him never thought other than that he did it and was it as a man.

In fact, almost the earliest falsification of the Gospel with which the first Christians had to contend was the suggestion that Jesus had been a heavenly being, not really human like the rest of us, and they resisted it vehemently. 'Many deceivers have gone out into the world, people who do not acknowledge Jesus Christ as coming in the flesh. Any such person is the deceiver and anti-Christ.' That was written in about AD 90, nearly 60 years after the death of Jesus.

So those contemporaries of Jesus who were drawn to become his followers knew him as a man, thought of him as a man, but clearly a man of God, an agent of God's kingship. And the Gospels make it clear that this is how Jesus also thought of himself. He was dependent on God; he prayed to God. In calling God his Father he was simply expressing the intense intimacy of his relationship with God and his commitment to model his human behaviour on the nature of the God he knew. If he thought the title 'Son of God' was applicable to himself, it is most probably because he knew that it had been given to Israel as God's people in the first place, so he may have thought of himself as the pioneer of a renewed Israel. If he saw himself as the Messiah, his acceptance of that designation was noticeably non-committal, and he certainly seems to have preferred the ambiguous term 'Son of Man' as a title because it was open to include others beside himself; it was an invitation to his followers to share the role with him, just as he called them to share his relationship with God. That is exactly what appears to have taken place. Their idea of God was being coloured by their growing acquaintance with this man. Their relationship to God was becoming inextricable from their relationship with him.

I think it is important to stress the personal hold that Jesus exercised over them as the key to our understanding of what happened, even though the language of sentiment would have been quite foreign to them. The word used in the Gospels is 'authority', which means, literally, what emanates from the inner being. There is no hint that what drew people to Jesus was a reputation for absolute goodness, still less any evidence of a supernatural prescience, which might have inspired fear, but not love. So arguments about his perfection, omniscience or omnipotence are beside the point and belong to a different era of discourse. His reputation as a healer certainly lured the crowds, but not for long. The impact he made on those who continued with him derived from a personality, a mind and a faith which compelled belief when he said that God and God's rule were now within their reach.

The appalling débâcle of his death should have shattered their emerging new image of God. It is nonsense to claim that the crucifixion of Jesus reveals the love of God. What it does demonstrate is the extraordinary loyalty to his ideals of a man who was put to death for the cause and the convictions he believed in. Call that love if you like – a man's love for truth or for justice, or even a man's love for God. But God is deafeningly absent, unless … unless we make the equation which those followers of Jesus made when they became convinced that he was more alive than ever, closer to them, yet more inseparably one with God than they had dared to conceive. He who had shown God to them now showed himself to them and they could never again think or speak of God without thinking and speaking of Jesus.

That equation, that inextricable coupling of the man Jesus with the God he had called Father, is reiterated in the earliest Christian document we possess, Paul's first letter to the Christians of Thessalonica, written, according to most New Testament scholars, no more than twenty years after the death of Jesus. Paul addresses the Christians as 'those who are in, or belong to, God the Father and the Lord Jesus Christ'. He prays: 'May our God and Father himself and our Lord Jesus bring us direct to you.' He urges them to rejoice and give thanks, adding, 'This is what God in Christ wills for you.'

Paul was a Jew who had a strict rabbinical training. Most of the first leaders of the new movement were Jews. So the New Testament authors were at pains to distinguish between the Risen Lord and the God who had raised him, between the one who was sent and the one who had sent him. Yet now the two belong to the same transcendent and eternal mode of being. Five years after that earliest letter, Paul is writing his first letter to the church at Corinth about the gods of the pagan world: 'There are many such gods and many such lords, yet for us there is one God the Father from whom are all things and we exist for him, and there is one Lord Jesus Christ through whom are all things and we exist through him.' For the first generation of Christians who had experienced God in Jesus, it was not an unthinkable step to feel that his exaltation to the transcendent realm was in some sense a return or homecoming.

As the new faith spread across Europe and began to adapt its gospel to classical thought, its more intellectual missionaries and pastors had to look for ways of reconciling the original and inalienable testimony of the relation between Jesus and God to the inflexible definitions of divinity which prevailed. The task engrossed and troubled the church for the next five centuries and more. But, in view of their insistence on his humanity, I think it is more natural to discern in the New Testament itself the germination of all the essentials of the doctrine of the incarnation than to fish around for such red herrings as Jewish archangels, Roman demi-gods and Samaritan gnostics to account for it.

Those three exotic suggestions were advanced in a book called *The Myth of God Incarnate*.[1] Since it seems that finding the right word is still a matter for debate, I would like to share a few thoughts on the implications of the word 'myth'.

Myth is a kind of poetry by which the significance of things is brought out. Most cultures have their creation myths and their myths of the End also. The first chapter of Genesis, to take one example, affirms mythologically that this hierarchical universe, culminating in humanity, has received its being through the initiating, activating purpose of God. If we choose to recognize the birth stories of Jesus as myth also, we could say that Luke's story of the annunciation is affirming the same thing: within the natural process of this birth that is to take place lies the initiating, activating purpose of God – 'the power of the Most High shall overshadow thee'. Indeed, I wonder whether we should ever have interpreted Luke's rather ambiguous story in the way we do had we never read Matthew's quite different myth, the point of which seems to be that Jesus is the fulfilment of prophecy.

---

[1] *The Myth of God Incarnate*, ed. John Hick, SCM Press 1977.

This, at any rate, has been the normal meaning of the word 'myth'. We can see the first two chapters of Genesis as creation myths, but what they affirm, whether we think it true or not, should not be described as myth. The affirmation of God's essential part in the coming into being of the universe, or the coming into being of Jesus Christ, is not mythological. It means just what it says.

It can mean what it says, however, only to those who, on the strength of their undeniable experiences, accept a 'two-storey' or 'two-story' version of all truth; those who believe, with the Jewish philosopher Martin Buber, that reality is sometimes knowable simply as an 'It', and sometimes comes to you as a 'Thou'; those who, having in one brief instant seen the world alight with an intense inner radiance and who, refusing to dismiss the experience as a subjective aberration, know that that glory is the greater truth of it. For them the immanence of God is self-evident, though they respect his incognito and ask only for enough faith to go on seeing the invisible. But it seems to me that those who can accept only a one-storey or one-story version of reality are trapped in a positivist set of Chinese boxes, wherein the truth that any one myth affirms turns out to be only another myth itself, leaving them with no more than a myth of God.

God was in Christ in the same way in which God is in the whole process of creation, though we should add that there are differences of degree in the interpenetration by God of God's creatures, and in the person of Jesus it became a complete identification. God's eternal commitment to God's purpose of love, God's Word of delight and dedication, God's 'Yes', was translated, accurately and dramatically, into the totally other language of a human life, into the 'Yes' of Jesus of Nazareth.

Recognition of the divine in that human life came gradually to those who began to love him. It came through the pull of his person and the change he wrought in them. But as they tried to tell others of that experience, those who heard were captivated and transformed in the same way. The recognition and the change are still happening, which is why we can speak of a living Christ. The first letter of Peter sums up this extraordinary phenomenon: 'You have not seen him, yet you love him; and trusting in him now without seeing him, you are filled with a glorious joy too great for words.'

8

And God Raised Him Up

Within a few weeks of the assassination of Mahatma Gandhi in 1948, every Indian store all over East Africa, even at the remotest crossing of two bush paths, displayed several glossy coloured posters, showing the familiar, domed-headed, bespectacled figure seated in the posture of holy meditation. And in most of these pictures the crucified Christ was portrayed faintly behind him. These posters were not designed for Christians but for ordinary Indians all over the world. Hinduism could find no other symbol to express its ultimate word about Gandhi.

One of the most notable of contemporary Arabic poets is the Palestinian nationalist Mahmoud Darwish. Like many Arab writers he is anguished over the apparent indifference of God towards the protracted weakness and suffering of the Islamic nations. Again and again in his verses he also employs the same symbol to protest at the tearing apart of his land:

> I was not the first to carry a crown of thorns
> That I should say: Let me weep.
> Could it be that my cross is a steed,
> And the thorns engraved on my brow
> In blood and sweat are a laurel crown?

The Jewish author, Chaim Potok, in his novel, *My Name is Asher Lev*, tells the story of a young painter torn between the faith of his fathers and the calling of his art. His father's life-work has been devoted to the rescue of refugee Jews and the strengthening of Jewish communities in many places. The artist recalls how much time his mother has spent at the window of their Brooklyn apartment, watching for her husband's return and, later, for his own return also from the Gentile world of Paris. And he paints a canvas of her in her housecoat, fixed to the vertical wooden divide of that window, her arms stretched along the slanting base of the Venetian blind a few inches from the top of the window. Her thin body is arched and her head twisted. On her right stands her husband in a hat and coat, carrying an attaché case. Opposite him is her son, in paint-spattered clothes, with a palette and a long spearlike brush.

> For all the pain you suffered, my mama. For all the torment of your past and future years, my mama. For all the anguish this picture of pain will cause you. For the unspeakable mystery that brings good fathers and sons into the world and lets a mother watch them tear at each other's throats. For the Master of the Universe, whose suffering world I do not comprehend. For dreams of horror, for nights of waiting, for memories of death, for the love I have for you, for all the things I remember, and for all the things I should remember but have forgotten, for all these I created this painting – an observant Jew working on a crucifixion because there was no aesthetic mould in his own religious tradition into which he could pour a painting of ultimate anguish and torment.[1]

Such deeply moving recourse to the symbol of the crucified Christ occurs again and again in many different situations today. Compared with the Christian interpretation of the cross one may feel that these examples are near and yet so far. Jesus crucified is here the supreme symbol of life sacrificed for others, or for truth. He is the archetype of all victims of oppression whose endurance will in the end win the triumph of justice. Or he simply sums up the whole tale of the world's incomprehensible pain. What is missing from these interpretations of the cross is the universal embrace of forgiveness or the redemption of the oppressors through the death of the victim. Yet even without these insights, the choice of this symbol in preference to any others is remarkable.

Why was this martyr taken as the inspiration of a new movement with a new conception of God's relation to the world, rather than the seven brothers whose torture and heroic death for the faith were popularized in the second book of Maccabees at about the same date as Jesus? And in an age that confronts us with the ovens of Dachau and the cinders of Hiroshima and the cells of Santiago or Robben

---

[1] Chaim Potok, *My Name is Asher Lev*, Heinemann 1972; Penguin 1974, pp. 287–8.

Island, why should people feel that that one bygone execution still speaks the last, inclusive word? Yet they do.

The reason must surely be that the crucifixion of Jesus Christ is seen by everyone of whatever faith surrounded by the aura with which Christian theology has invested it. It cannot be separated from the preaching of the cross. The Christian interpretation of that death may be only partially grasped. It may be partially rejected. Yet the idea persists that there is something godlike about it. It is known from the start as a disclosure of ultimate meaning, either about God or about man, or both.

But to say this only shifts the problem to another point. Where did the Christian theology come from? Why wasn't this death the end of the story and the fall of the curtain on the whole movement? The only answer, I believe, is the resurrection. To know that he who had died that death was alive and present added a new dimension to all that Jesus of Nazareth had been and had suffered. It raised to a totally different scale the question that had already disturbed their orthodoxy: 'Who do you say that I am?' The simple conviction that God had roused up and raised up Jesus from the dead not only vindicated his gospel of the kingdom, it gave it an immediacy it could not have before this event. The salvation and victory of that kingdom no longer lay in a veiled future; it had arrived, and arrived in the person of that Risen One. The proclamation of the kingdom must from thenceforth become a proclaiming of his death and resurrection.

The German New Testament scholar Rudolf Bultmann and those who still follow him have given a different account. They suggest that, so far from the experience of the resurrection giving rise to the theological interpretation of the life and death of Jesus, it was the other way round. Reflection on the death of Jesus brought them to realize its profound spiritual significance, a significance and a power which must 'live on'. To believe in the resurrection is simply to admit that the death of Jesus has saving power *for me*. Jesus, said Bultmann, had risen in the proclamation of the Good News.

But where was the Good News if the historical event of Jesus of Nazareth ended with the burial of his body? It is the story of an individual passion for God and for the rule of freedom and truth and for the vindication of the weak and outcast, a passion sustained unfaltering and forgiving to the end. It is a triumph of human aspiration and love, perhaps supreme. But as to what it assures us

about the nature of God, we might very well conclude with
Aeschylus that 'the President of the Immortals had ended his sport'.

Reflection on the death of a martyr may lead to a conviction that
resurrection is promised to him at the end of time. This was how men
responded to the death of the seven brothers recorded in the second
book of Maccabees. 'The King of the Universe will raise us up to a life
everlastingly made new.' That was a theological breakthrough, and at
the time of Jesus people were still speculating uncertainly as to
whether it was to be trusted, and in what manner it might be realized.
But the claim that the eschatological resurrection had in one man's
case taken place within the ongoing course of history was un-
precedented and could in no wise have been deduced by reflection on
his godforsaken death. Something else must have given rise to that
unparalleled belief.

There is no way of proving that God raised Jesus from the dead.
Even should fresh evidence confirm the empty tomb or the
appearances of the Risen Lord, these incidents in themselves would
be open to more than one interpretation. Making God the subject of
any sentence is the language of faith; it is a theological interpretation
of an event. Providence is always transparent; if you will, you can
invariably look through it to another, purely natural or human
agency. And yet it is given us to know that the hand of God was at
work in these events. That knowledge, that disclosure of meaning, is
not strictly historical, but neither can it be independent of history. In
order to arrive at a theological interpretation of an event you must
have an event to interpret.

'The Lord is risen and has appeared to Simon.' There you have it in
the two parts of that early formula: the unprovable assertion of faith,
'roused and raised', and the fact, whatever it means, 'appeared, seen'.
Just as, in the story of the first creation, God's *fiat lux* (theology) is
linked with 'There was light' (historical phenomenon). Just as body
and blood are linked with bread and wine.

He appeared. He was seen. That was the tradition handed down.
There is a 'happened-ness' in Easter which turned utter darkness into
a blaze of light. Looking at the cross in that light, we can affirm that
God was in Christ, reconciling the world to himself. It is the fact of
his resurrection that makes the fact of his death universally significant
and redemptive.

9

The Easter God

The Sunday after Easter used to be called 'Low Sunday'. After the excitement of Easter, with its inflated turnout of strangers in the congregation, this was anticlimax. The vicar had taken the Easter offering and gone for his spring holiday, leaving a frightened curate or inaudible retired priest to celebrate for a handful of regulars. Low Sunday indeed, the slump after the boom.

And that was an accurate reflection of what the followers of Jesus must have been feeling on that very first Sunday after Easter, when they began to wonder whether they were still '*in Easter*' after all.

It was already turning into a confused memory of rumours, terror and mounting excitement. Breathless women had woken them with a babble of angels by an empty tomb. Later on Peter himself verified that much, but without the angels. Next Mary Magdalene claimed actually to have seen the Lord for an instant and someone or other believed Peter had done the same. By the evening, when two friends from the country turned up saying they had recognized Jesus briefly at their own supper-table, the mixture of fear and expectation had boiled over – and there he was, visible to them all, greeting them as though nothing had changed.

But that was a week ago and nothing like it had happened since. They had shared their experiences with a few trusted friends, but as the days passed you can imagine the look in their eyes, the raised eyebrows, especially those of their fellow-apostle, the one they knew as 'The Twin', Thomas.

Thomas was always the pessimist – 'realist', he called it. He was never carried away by excitement, nor by fear. And yet his feelings ran deep, deeper perhaps than anyone's. Earlier, when Jesus had announced his intention to go back into the dangers of Judaea for the sake of their friend Lazarus who had died, it was Thomas who

said: 'Let us go too, that we may die *with* him.' For Thomas is a man
who offers no hope when there is none, and will not profess a faith he
hasn't got, but will die for the love he does have. You can trust him
because he takes nothing for granted. So during the Last Supper,
when Jesus said to the disciples, 'You know the way I am taking',
Thomas dares to object: 'We don't even know where you're going;
how can we know the way?'

This down-to-earth, inwardly sensitive man cannot forget the
horror of Jesus's death. No rumoured hope or wild hallucination can
erase those raw wounds from his mind's eye. 'Show me those and I'll
know I am dealing with reality, the only reality there is now – and it
can't be reconciled with a living Lord.'

So there they were, like us, on Low Sunday, after a week in which
not a thing had happened to confirm the truth of those fleeting
appearances of Easter Day. Was Thomas right, after all, to doubt their
stories? And if we were as honest as he was, might we not doubt them
too? After Easter, the world does not suddenly change, and it is
difficult, isn't it, trying to reconcile all those alleluias with what we see
day by day on our TV screens? What's more, we look back across not
one week but 2000 years of blatantly unredeemed human history
since Jesus died to save the world. So what sort of victory have we
been celebrating?

Let Thomas the realist answer that question.

First of all, Easter celebrates the simple commonplace victories of
human love. It doesn't need to be religious, yet it's stronger than
death, greater than faith or hope. The death of Jesus destroyed the
hopes of his followers yet, like Mary Magdalene, they still loved the
dead man. Thomas had foreseen that death, yet offered a love that was
ready to die. In fact he had run away like the others, but it was that
love and its failure that tortured him now with such violent disbelief.

It's love, more than faith, that Jesus asks for. It's love that he
inspires, and faith grows out of that love. There are dark times when I
can believe in God only because that man did, and I'd rather be
deluded with him than right in any other company. But remember,
this absurd persistence in loving long after the loved one has been
taken away by death or mental collapse is not limited to religious
people. It is implanted in our human nature, part of the likeness of
God we all carry within us.

But the next victory that Easter calls us to celebrate is a victory over
time and space. After six days with no sign of a Risen Christ, they

were all together again, including Thomas. (Thank God for a church which makes the agnostic feel at home!) And suddenly Jesus was there, giving his familiar greeting. Then, turning at once to Thomas, he answered what Thomas had asked six days before, as if the words had just been spoken. 'All right, Thomas, if that's what you need, reach out and feel my wounds and get rid of your doubts.' Thomas's brain must have reeled. 'Was he there when I said that? What else has he heard? And who else?' Thomas might have recalled the words of Psalm 139: 'Thou understandest my thought afar off ... for there is not a word on my tongue, but lo! O Lord, thou knowest it altogether.' But to whom was that ancient psalm addressed? What man, even one risen from the dead, could be so everywhere and, at the same time, so intimately here and now? To these whirling questions Thomas blurts out the only possible answer: 'My Lord and my God!'

Yet there, within inches of his finger-tips, are the wounds which have been haunting Thomas's imagination. Can they ever be reconciled with those words he had just spoken? They can. And this is the supreme victory which we celebrate at Easter, the truth revealed through the cross and resurrection of Jesus. It is the victory of God's persistence in love. This is the truth that is being reflected, as I said, in the dogged persistence of human beings, in spite of the pain it perpetuates, in loving someone who has died or gone away.

Tragically, we humans persist also in self-will, which is the opposite of love, so that our TV screens display more of our inhumanity than our likeness to God, and the scenes which distress us are raw wounds to God. The victory of his endurance lies in his eternal commitment never to switch off love.

Just after the First World War, the poet Edward Shillito wrote:

> The other gods were strong, but thou wast weak;
> They rode, but thou didst stumble to a throne.
> But to our wounds only God's wounds can speak,
> And not a God has wounds, but thou alone.[1]

Paul's great hymn to God's love in the thirteenth chapter of his first

---

[1] Edward Shillito (1872–1948), from 'Jesus of the Scars'. The quotation was made famous by William Temple, who used it in his *Readings in St John's Gospel*, 1939.

letter to the Corinthians does not say that love always wins, but that there is no limit to its faith, its hope, its endurance, and that love will never come to an end. For all who know the love of Christ that is promise enough, and worthy of all our alleluias.

10

The Self-Giving God

Then he breathed on them, saying, 'Receive the Holy Spirit.' (John 20.22)

What does it mean when we call God 'Holy Spirit'? For that matter, what do we mean when we call God 'Father'? Or when we call God 'Son'? It is all the same God we are talking about. There aren't three Gods, nor can God be divided into three parts. When we read that on the day of Pentecost they were all filled with the Holy Spirit we could just as truly say they were all filled with God.

Being human is something we do know about. Being a tree is something we find difficult to imagine. Being God is utterly beyond our comprehension. Yet a little of the mystery has been shown to us. Within God's own self God is love. We know about relationship, about love, through our contacts with other beings outside ourselves. God's way of being differs totally from ours by including the knowledge of relationship within itself.

That is truly beyond our power of imagination and we had better not pretend otherwise. But we can at least see that it does make sense if we remember how, in our own loving, our own self-giving, we do as individuals contain several identities which are distinct in their awareness of themselves and their relation to each other.

Think of the various types of absolute self-giving which we may meet in our world: Mother Teresa's dedication to the destitute in Calcutta; Martin Luther King's self-sacrifice for the liberation of the black community in America; Stephen Hawking's total devotion to uncovering some of the mystery of the universe; Barbara Hepworth's striving to express in sculpture her vision of the spiritual energy that blows within rocks or trees or clouds; Thomas Merton's lifelong quest for the vision of God; or any mother who is living for her children. In each of them there is the born self-giver who can find fulfilment only in some form of outgoing, self-spending purpose, and is wholly absorbed in willing its achievement, whether that be the welcome of the destitute, the dream of an integrated society, the well-being of the children, or whatever. Ask all those self-giving people why they pursue such a purpose and they can in honesty give no other answer than 'That's how I am.' And this may be a faint clue suggesting how we should think of the self-giving nature and changeless purpose in God which we define as the Father but who names himself, 'I am what I am.'

But there is another way in which all those self-giving people that I named can be aware of themselves. They are the selves that are being given, sacrificed for the liberation of their people, for the work of art. Behind them, as it were, is the changeless decision of their nature which they must obey. They are men and women under orders to the purpose they have set themselves, and they think of themselves as serving a cause, answering a call, fulfilling a task, or responding to an inner drive. Ask them why they persevere and, in this mode of self-awareness, they reply, not 'I am', but 'I must'.

And this is precisely the language which the Bible ascribes to the self-given-ness of God's nature as it responds to the imperative of God's changeless purpose, which is what we mean by 'God the Son'. For obedience to his own purpose is not something alien to God, and when God the Son became incarnate in obedience to that purpose he used the language of response and vocation: 'The Son can do nothing on his own account but only what he sees the Father doing.' 'I must give the good news of the kingdom of God to the other towns also for that is what I was sent to do.' That is the voice of God obeying the dictates of his own self-giving will.

But think again of Mother Teresa, Stephen Hawking, Martin Luther King, of the sculptress, the seeker after God, the mother. The final stage of their self-giving is a merging of the self with the object of their devotion. The mother so identifies her own being with the lives of her children, the scientist has so entered into the mysterious realm he is exploring the artist is so at one with her work of art, as to know them from the inside and be fulfilled only in their fulfilment. Ask them now why they are pouring out their energies in this way and they will not answer, 'I am such and such', nor 'I must this or that', for they have lost sight of themselves entirely. Instead they will speak of their sheer delight in the worth of the other. Mother Teresa will say, 'See how peacefully this old man dies.' Hawking may say, 'See how beautifully, how miraculously this equation works out.' Martin

Luther King will describe his dream. The mystic will have no words to tell what he has caught a glimpse of. For all of them the given self has become the in-othered self. The first Christian hermit, St Antony, used to repeat: 'My life and my death is in my neighbour', and the more you think about them, the more you will be astonished by the truth of those words.

The final stage of God's self-giving also is God's in-othering, God's total empathy, God's delight and fulfilment in the other to whom he gives himself, so that God knows that other from the inside. We are dealing with a Creator who so gives himself to his creation that he has entered into the very heart of each thing he has made. Not a sparrow falls without God falling with it. And it is this culmination of God's self-giving, God in his entering-in, that we call the Holy Spirit.

Spiritus means a breath of air. So does the Greek *pneuma*, which we also translate as 'spirit'. So does the Hebrew *ruach*, which is used in the Old Testament both for the wind and the Spirit of God. And if we speak of the Holy Ghost we are using a word with the same origin as gust. The Holy Ghost is a holy gust of the wind of God. 'Breathe on me, Breath of God.' It is a marvellous metaphor.

The invisible air that brushes your cheek is the same air that extends beyond the farthest clouds and bears up the highest flying plane. It enfolds the whole earth and without that embrace this would be a lifeless planet. Such is the transcendence of the Creator. Yet, entering you on every breath you take, it refreshes and renews your being and, exhaled, it takes with it your stale impurities so that breathing itself is a continuous absolution. And this the air is doing for me too and for every other thing that has breath. Such is the immanence, the within-ness, of God. To say 'Where can I find God?' is like asking 'Where is this atmosphere they keep talking about?' You are in it and it is in you. So also God is Spirit, breath, in whom we live and move and have our being. The wind blows where it wills, and how it wills, whether as a cool caress or a hurricane, such is God's unpredictability. Yet God is not impersonal like the wind. God's touch is a real caress, God's enveloping of all things is truly an embrace, and God's entering into all things is the culmination of an actual self-giving whereby he becomes one with the object of his love. In all our moments of special aliveness God is delighting within us, in all our affliction he is afflicted, and when we are most truly in prayer we become aware that we are being prayed through by a voice and a will that is greater than our own.

If we accept God's in-othering, if we co-operate with God's sharing of our experiences from within us, we shall find that he gives us the same power of identifying with others, becoming aware of their feelings from the inside, responding as we would like them to respond to us – in other words, bearing one another's burdens. This is the genuine pentecostal gift which on the first Whit Sunday enabled every person in that crowd of many races to hear the Gospel as though it were addressed to them individually in their own language. So the self-giving, self-given God, by filling us with himself, creates a self-giving, self-given people that reaches out and out, ever wider, until it embraces all creation and the great purpose of God is realized.

11

The Nature of God

There are two ways of being aware of God which are often contrasted: either God out there, in a dimension beyond space and time, or God the guiding reality at the core of my being.

These two traditions of thinking about God seem to be related to two quite common types of experience, which are incontrovertible to those who receive them. One, called *numinous* experience, is like an encounter initiated by some reality or presence beyond oneself. Here are two recorded examples. One relates: 'I kind of knew this was something extraordinary at the moment it occurred. It was as simple as that, just seeing these trees.' Another wrote: 'The sky was, I might almost say, looking at me. A mutual awareness was happening between myself and an overwhelming presence.'

It isn't difficult to see that such 'I–Thou' experiences of encounter and response were the root from which grew the three great faiths with a Semitic origin – Judaism, Christianity and Islam. But it was the other main type of transcendental experience which laid the foundation of Indo-Aryan religion. This is *mystical* experience, the essence of which is a moment of illumination in which one recognizes that one's own inmost self is at one with the unity of all things. I quote again, first from a woman who described how she had discovered as a child 'not so much a sense of self-awareness as of absorption in something far greater than myself of which I was at the same time a part and glad and grateful to be so'. And again, from a young man who says, 'It was as if a switch marked "Ego" was suddenly switched off. I was the sunset and there was no "I" experiencing "it", no more observer and observed.'

Again it is easy to see how it was compelling illuminations such as these that gave birth to the Hindu perception of *a-dvaita*, non-duality, the conviction that all impressions of 'otherness' are illusory and that when I penetrate to my true inmost being I find it is none other than Being itself, the eternal I AM, residing indivisible in all that is.

The two ways of being aware of God do seem to be mutually contradictory. That in itself doesn't justify rejecting either of them. What does deserve rejection is the current trivializing of both these traditions of thought about God and human identity. The mystery of God's objective otherness is being invoked to present him familiarly as a fellow being among other beings, though no doubt the greatest. Objective otherness likewise reduces *my* identity to the level of a product: I am what other people and events out there – my parents, my traumatic experiences – have made me. Meanwhile the alternative tradition of interiority is also being trivialized by reducing the mystery of the God within to a personified ideal or the coherence, such as it is, of my personal values. We have to reject these shallow alternatives and launch out into the deep, taking seriously both ways of being aware of God, since each needs the other to bring out and illumine its full significance.

That was certainly the driving conviction of the friend about whom I want to say a little. He saw that the Hindu tradition of identifying the search for God with the search for one's inmost self 'compels the Christian to become far more consciously and attentively aware of the interior dimensions of his own spiritual tradition'.

He was a Frenchman called Henri le Saux, born in 1910. At the age of 21 he became a Benedictine monk. After the Second World War he went to South India where, during his first two years of study, he came to know a remarkable Hindu holy man and spiritual guide, Sri Ramana. This man could illuminate the truth of *a-dvaita* – the indivisible identity of God with the inmost self of each person – because he had experienced it dramatically at the age of 16 before ever he found it spelled out in the Hindu scriptures. Henri le Saux told that story in more than one of the books he wrote later, and he could not have lit upon a humbler, holier or more enlightening guide into the Hindu vision of the God within.

When Sri Ramana died towards the end of Henri's second year in India, Henri and a colleague established in the same Tamil country an ashram, a household devoted, as in the Indian tradition, to the spiritual search in a lifestyle of simplicity and hospitality. They wore the saffron robes of Indian monks and took Sanskrit names. From that time Henri le Saux was forgotten, and he was known universally as Swami Abhishiktānanda, which means 'the bliss of the Christ'.

After seven years his first companion at the ashram also died, and Abhishiktānanda became more like one of the wandering holy men of India, the *sanyasis*, dividing his time between the ashram and a hermitage he built for himself at Gyansu, a village in the Himalayas towards the source of the Ganges.

I have referred to him as my friend, which is presumptuous, I suppose, since I met him only once for the inside of a week at another ashram in North India. I had gone there for some quiet and discussion after a huge and hectic international conference in Delhi. I have a photograph of him in his orange robe, chopping vegetables for the common meal, and another of us side by side in the bicycle-rickshaw that took us to the railway station, where we parted. What I remember is a man who was entirely ordinary yet unforgettable. He had immense depth, but it was all transparent; there were no barriers left in him.

Abhishiktānanda had changed his name, his dress, his mode of life; but this did not signify any surrender of his Christian faith. On the contrary, he found it was more fully confirmed. For he saw that the insights which the Spirit of God had entrusted long before to the seers and sages of India could become in these days the corrective that the church needs to save it from the trivializing of its own traditions. For he himself had had the transforming illumination to which the holy sages of India bore witness – the steady putting aside of all those false identities that people and events impose upon us, and the fantasy selves in which our frightened ego clothes itself, until he had penetrated to the very 'cave of the heart' or 'place of welling up', as the Upanishads call it, and recognized his 'real me', the true mystery of the person, and heard at last that authentic 'I am' of self-awareness which was indistinguishable from the eternal I AM of God, the Beyond at the centre within. Not the platitudinous 'divine spark', which sounds so very shut-in, but a trap-door at the heart of everything which proves to be a skylight opening out to the radiance of infinity.

How then did Abhishiktānanda reconcile this experience with the Christian, Jewish, Muslim sense of God's incomparable transcendence? By looking more profoundly at, of all things, the Christian doctrine of the Trinity!

When he and his colleague established their spiritual household in South India they called it the *Saccidānanda* ashram. The name is a combination of three Hindu terms. *Sat* means simply Being, Is-ness. It expresses the mystery of anything's existence, but especially the divine Brahman – God within himself, of which we can know nothing but that he is. *Cit*, the second term, means awareness, consciousness. So the combination *Saccit* describes awareness of being oneself, recognition of, and contact with, one's true self. And the freedom from self-concern, the fulfilment, the bliss which flows from that state of integration is *ānanda*. Abhishiktānanda grasped the striking correspondence between those three terms, *Sat-cit-ānanda,* and the Christian perception of God as Trinity. God as pure Being, the essence of existence as such and source of all beings. God the Father, the Source, is beyond human sight and comprehension. God's comprehension of himself, God's self-awareness, his self-naming, is what we mean by the Word, the Son. The bliss, or as Christians would say, the communication of love, which flows from the mutuality between self and self-awareness, is God the Creator Spirit.

In one of his books Abhishiktānanda has said:

> God's presence to himself and his presence to me, these two mysteries cannot be separated. In the last resort God's presence in me or to me is nothing else than his presence to himself. The 'Thou' he addresses to me is the 'Thou' he addresses to the beloved Son, and it is only in my identity with the Son which he has given me that I can say, Abba, Father.

Or, in Paul's words from his letter to the Galatians, 'God sent forth the Spirit of his Son into our hearts, our inmost reality, crying, Abba, Father.'

That inmost reality of simply being, with all mental images of oneself stripped away, is the cave of the heart, where the ultimate reality that is Beyond wells up within. In the story told by John in the fourth chapter of his Gospel of the Samaritan woman drawing water at the well, the woman objected to the promise Jesus had just made: 'You've no container, no bucket, and the well is deep. How can you give me this living, running water?' And, in so many words, his answer was: 'I'm not offering you a cupful or a bucketful from this external source, but an inexhaustible spring at the centre of your own being welling up with life eternally.'

When we learn to hold that inner reality of ourselves open to what is wholly other and beyond, as we do when listening to the greatest music, we may begin to hear, resounding everywhere, the divine self-announcement, I AM, and with it, small and clear, more like an echo than another voice, our own 'I am'. That is the essence of prayer. That is what we are made for.

12

The Forgiveness of God

Were you not bound to have pity on your fellow servant,
just as I had pity on you? (Matthew 18.33)

The answer was obviously, 'No, not at all.' He didn't feel bound to have
mercy. He wasn't living in the same moral world as his generous master.
No one can be *obliged* to show mercy. Shylock, in Shakespeare's *The
Merchant of Venice*, knew that. When Portia, disguised as a young
barrister, recognizes the validity of the bond which the debtor, Antonio,
has signed, she says, 'Then must the Jew be merciful.' Shylock retorts,
'On what compulsion must I? Tell me that.' And she has to admit, 'The
quality of mercy is not strained'; not constrained, obligatory.

This was the real issue between Jesus and the Pharisees. They too
believed, just as he did, in God's forgiving acceptance of sinners, and
they strove to bring it about. But they saw it as a kind of contract
whereby the sinner must repent and mend his ways and prove it by
making restitution, and, on the strength of this, be assured of divine
forgiveness. Whereas for Jesus it meant being transferred into a
different moral realm altogether, the kingdom of God, where the laws
of just deserts, reward and penalty, did not apply, but a spontaneous
exchange of love. Either that kingdom had become your home or it
was still beyond your comprehension. Many Christians even now,
when they read the Gospels, are puzzled to see how he who knew
better than all others the true cost of forgiveness could apparently
dispense it so lightly to individual sinners.

The Christian novelist Charles Williams threw a fascinating light
on that puzzle in a small book called *The Forgiveness of Sins*,[1] published

---

[1] Reissued Faber 1980.

just as the Second World War was coming to an end. He pointed to
the way in which Shakespeare dealt with forgiveness at different stages
in his career as a dramatist. First he looked at Shakespeare's earliest
play, *The Two Gentlemen of Verona*. The two gentlemen having
demonstrated the ease with which they can both switch their
affections, Shakespeare wants to get the company off-stage in a happy
ending before the wretched pair change their minds once more! The
less guilty one, however, is still an outlaw, together with his band of
thieves. But the Duke solves that problem in a cursory couplet:

> Thou hast prevailed. I pardon them and thee.
> Dispose of them as thou know'st their deserts.

Such forgiveness is a mere convenience: 'Let's say no more about it.'
It trivializes the relationship of the characters concerned, so that, as
Charles Williams put it, 'for all the interest we have in them they
might as well have been executed at once'.

Measure for Measure was written at the height of Shakespeare's
powers during 1604, three years after *Hamlet* and in the same year as
Othello. Whatever his religious convictions may have been, his
handling of forgiveness in this play shows a profound understanding
of the insights of the gospel. In this plot a genuine, but over-austere
idealist, who has just been unexpectedly called to deputize as head of
state, falls prey to lust for a young novice in a convent. Even so the
story only works if his passion for morality is taken seriously.

> O cunning enemy, that to catch a saint
> With saints dost bait thy hook!

It happens that the young novice's brother is under sentence of
death (according to their law) for having intercourse with his
sweetheart before marriage, and when the novice comes from her
convent to plead for his life with the deputy ruler, he offers her the
pardon only in exchange for her consent to his lust. But having, as he
thinks, spent a night with her (though, in Shakespearean fashion, it
was actually someone else), he still orders her brother's execution to
ensure that his evil bargain should never come to light. At that point
the true head of state reappears as judge, having watched these
hypocritical acts in secret. And now the full Christian theology of
contrition and restoration is acted out. Angelo, the guilty moralist,
sees himself for what he is in the eyes of divine justice and begs for
punishment:

> Let my trial be mine own confession:
> Immediate sentence then and sequent death
> Is all the grace I beg.

He is condemned to execution. His wife pleads for his pardon and asks the young novice, Isabella, to plead alongside her. So, after an inward struggle – for she still supposes her brother has been put to death – Isabella kneels and intercedes:

> Look, if it please you, on this man condemned
> As if my brother lived. I partly think
> A due sincerity govern'd his deeds
> 'Til he did look on me: since it is so,
> Let him not die. My brother had but justice
> In that he did the thing for which he died:
> For Angelo,
> His act did not o'ertake his bad intent.

In her very words we can hear the faint but unmistakable echo, first of the repentant thief on Calvary and then of Christ himself: 'Forgive them, for they know not what they do.'

It has often been pointed out that in the four romances of Shakespeare's last phase forgiveness is the final resolution towards which each complicated plot finds its way and comes to rest. Yet, when it is reached, that forgiveness is almost as perfunctory as in the earliest comedy. To his usurping brother, Prospero, in *The Tempest*, says merely, 'I do forgive thy rankest fault; all of them.' And when the second of his enemies speaks of the need for forgiveness, he interrupts him:

> There, sir, stop;
> Let us not burden our remembrances
> With a heaviness that's gone.

When, in *The Winter's Tale*, Hermione is once again face to face with the husband who so insanely wronged her, and when Imogen, in *Cymbeline*, confronts the madly jealous husband who had hired an assassin to kill her, they do not speak a word of their forgiveness: the joy of their silent embrace says it all. And that is the point. That is what makes the forgiveness in these last plays of Shakespeare most like the forgiveness of Jesus in the Gospels, which the Pharisees considered far too casual.

Having brought out this point, Charles Williams said: 'There is a tendency among some Christians to overdo forgiveness as they overdo patience and other virtues.' And he went on: 'Love, we have been told, is slow to anger. It is, as a result, slow to forgive, for it will not be in a hurry to assume that there is anything to forgive.'

Jesus Christ was forgiveness incarnate. In his flesh and blood he embodied the eternally forgiving heart of God. There was no question of his making light of sin, as the Pharisees suspected, for he knew the alienation it sets up and he was ready to pay the price of breaking through the barrier. Yet when he was face to face with one friend who had quite blatantly let him down, denying all knowledge of their old attachment, Jesus didn't seek an apology. He didn't mention forgiveness. He asked only, 'Do you love me? Do you love me really?'

That is God's way. The reconciliation he seeks with each of us, time after time as need be, is not casual. It touches the very depths of God's being and ours, beyond the reach of formulas, or any words, where only tears or something like costly perfume will say what needs to be said. For God's pardon is not so much a transaction as an embrace.

13

Being Transformed

How amazingly rich we are to have four Gospels, with three accounts of the transfiguration, for no one person's experience of Jesus Christ can be complete. We need one another's experiences and one another's way of seeing things. Luke's account comes in the ninth chapter of his Gospel, and it is different from the others. He sees the story through an artist's eye and with a doctor's diagnosis by looking to what is going on inside. And so he actually speaks not so much of an outward glory, that which the three disciples saw and which Mark and Matthew both dwell upon; rather, Luke tells us what is going on inwardly, in the experience of Jesus, and he brings out many of the similarities that there are with another experience which Jesus was yet to undergo.

It is Luke who tells us that Jesus came to the place with three others in order to pray, and it was while he was praying that it all happened. He also tells us, and only Luke does so, that they were heavy with sleep and that in Jesus' mind as he prayed was the thought of his departure which he had to accomplish in Jerusalem. And it is Luke who tells us that there were beings from beyond the earthly realm to strengthen him to face what was to come; not only Moses and Elijah, which the others mention, but later an angel as well. Yes, there is a link, there is a likeness with Gethsemane. Eight days before this transfiguration, Luke tells us, Jesus had first foretold what was to come: his sufferings and his death. And, as Matthew and Mark say, as they came down from the transfiguration experience, they were talking about his death.

So it seems that Luke is suggesting that what was going on inside Jesus was a crisis of commitment to what he knew must be. Luke doesn't deny the glory. He says since they stayed awake they saw his glory. So they did see it. But he doesn't use the word 'transfiguration'.

What he says is that the appearance of his face changed. And even that doesn't quite give the meaning of the Greek words. He simply says the appearance of his face was 'other'. It was different, and that is a phrase that could equally well be used of a face that was marred with sweat falling down like great drops of blood, which Luke alone mentions of all the evangelists.

The church that has been built by the Franciscans in this century on the summit of Mount Hermon, which some believe may have been the mountain of transfiguration, is brilliantly conceived, with two sanctuaries. There is one which you have to enter by flights of steps up the side of an archway where there are frescoes of the transfiguration, and it is called the Chapel of the Glorification. Below it is a flight of steps centrally which lead down into what is called the Chapel of the Humiliation, where there are frescoes of Gethsemane.

But if Luke's guess is right, and the inner experience of Jesus on that mountain was a foretaste of the agony that was to come in Gethsemane, was the disciples' vision of a shining glory unreal? To answer that question I think we must consider our own experiences of transfiguration, and they are frequent in all of us. You walk around a picture gallery, one perhaps that you have walked round before, but this time suddenly one picture stands out. It seems to come towards you, it grips you, you see a significance that you never saw before. Or you may be driving in the country and one vista, even if you have passed it many times, strikes and holds you. It is different. It is speaking to you. Or you may be reading a book. You may be reading the Bible and one sentence seems to be directed to you alone, with a meaning which you have never seen in it before, as in this passage of Luke perhaps.

When things light up, when things shine mysteriously, a transfiguration is taking place. It is unforgettable. It becomes part of you. It shines in you and from you and it is the gift of the Holy Spirit. This supremely, as I see it, is the gift of the Holy Spirit; the gift of awareness, bringing you alive, bringing you awake so that suddenly your senses grasp what is there which you never saw before and which others haven't noticed.

Since they had stayed awake, they saw his glory. There is only a man praying, wrestling in prayer on a mountain top; but now they became aware of the otherworldly companionship that was holding him up. They became aware of the Father's acceptance which was so real to him. They became aware of the underlying agony of loving obedience. What they became aware of, what we become aware of, we reflect, like Moses on his mountain top long before. He had said to God, 'Show me your glory. Let me see your glory', and God granted his prayer so that as he came down with the Law from God, his face shone with the glory he had been looking at. So Paul says to us: 'We are beholding as in a mirror' – the mirror of Jesus Christ – the glory of God shining out of his agony and suffering. We, beholding that, are transfigured from one glory to another, so that we shine. It's a hall of mirrors, if you like. Others may see in us what we have seen in Jesus, even though it shines out in agony – what Jesus sees in God.

14

The Coming of the Kingdom

If Christ be not raised your faith is vain, has nothing in it. (I Corinthians 15.17)

The Sunday after Easter, when numbers often drop to an all-time low following the big festival, seems a suitable day to look for a while into the depths of meaninglessness into which we might be plunged if – and it remains the greatest if of all time – Christ was not raised from the dead.

Rembrandt knew, better than all other painters, that in order to convey the brightness of light it is necessary to show the depth of the surrounding darkness. It is impossible to grasp the miracle of Easter unless one has looked steadily at the possibility that there was no resurrection.

The most sceptical among contemporary New Testament scholars and philosophers of religion are doing us at least the service of making us taste the horror of putting our faith in a Jesus whose story ended with his burial. For that horror was precisely the experience of his friends during the two nights and a day that followed his crucifixion.

What had they seen in Jesus? What was it that had captured their devotion and their hopes?

A man to whom God's fatherly presence was a continuous, intimate reality so close and direct as to displace the teachings and rituals and rules through which it seemed God had to be mediated to other people.

A man already convinced, like others, that the kingdom of the new age was about to dawn, who found in this overwhelmingly simple relationship that he knew with his Father the evidence that the new age, the kingdom of that Father, had already broken into history.

A man who therefore called all other men to live the life of the kingdom now in anticipation of its complete arrival, and to experience here and now the healing and the transformation and the freedom of the rule of God.

A man who came to see himself, because of the closeness of his relationship with God, as the one in whom the future kingdom was already being realized, and through whom it must be inaugurated.

A man who finally set his face to go up to Jerusalem, believing that he had to play out to the end the role of the Suffering Servant in order to be the Messiah. He invited the chosen twelve to drink this bitter cup with him. But if they could not, then he would drink it alone, if there was to be no other way. He would offer himself to death and await his vindication by the Father, which should throw open the doors of the kingdom and usher in the new creation.

That was the man whose vision and faith had captivated them, whose truth and spontaneity had won their commitment and whose trust they betrayed. From afar they watched, or heard, what happened.

His enemies sprung their trap. That was not surprising: he had more or less put himself into their hands. Integrity and justice had bent under strain: that also was usual. What was less expected was the ease with which the common people were turned against him and the violence of their hostility.

But it was not in them that his confidence rested, nor in the powers that be, nor even in the courage of his friends. His Father alone was the one in whom he put his trust. It was his Father who was giving him this cup to drink. That unbroken closeness of God would sustain him, and his perfect love of the Father would somehow be vindicated.

Yet, as the agony and shame of his dying dragged on, he might just as well have been the defiant thief on one of the other crosses for all the notice God seemed to take. There was no presence supporting him, only the silence with which heaven has stared back at its millions of victims, before and since. We can't be sure as to which of the familiar seven words were actually spoken from the cross, and which reflect the meditations of the early church. The only one about which there is almost no doubt, quoted in two Gospels and referred to in a third, is the loud cry of forsakenness and, according to the earliest account of his death, '*Lama Sabachtani*' were his last words. If that was the last thing that happened to Jesus of Nazareth, then his betrayal by Judas was nothing to his betrayal by God.

I simply cannot understand those who say that there is good news in such a tale. Heroism, yes, and faithfulness to a vision and a hope.

But what price hope if it be deluded? There have, of course, been martyrdoms a-plenty with no heavenly intervention. They breed faith rather than despair for one reason only: that we have grounds for believing that God is not indifferent and does in the end vindicate those who trust him. But what grounds have we for such a belief if Jesus went forsaken into a darkness from which there was no return?

It is being suggested that in the death of Jesus we see the triumph of love and learn to identify the being of God with that kind of love. But this statement needs examining. Exactly where do we see love in the crucifixion? If it is in Jesus's love for God it seems to have been singularly unrequited. In any case, what brought him to the cross was a passionate expectancy and a loyalty to truth rather than love itself. Or do we mean that on the cross we see Jesus's love for his disciples or for mankind? This is true *if* we believe that in that death the Son of God loved me and gave himself for me, or that God was in Christ reconciling the world to himself. But these are post-Easter beliefs. In the light of the resurrection we can recognize what is Godlike in the figure on the cross and see the ultimate sacrifice of love. But if he was just a man dying for his beliefs it is only very indirectly that he was doing it for his friends. Is it God's love, then, that triumphs at the crucifixion? If 'Why hast thou forsaken me' is indeed the last word of the story, I see no loving God in it and no future for anyone.

Nor could the disciples of Jesus have seen love on that Friday night, or the Saturday that followed, or on any day for the rest of time, unless something else had happened.

God was not to be trusted and all sense of meaning in the universe had collapsed into moral chaos. The earth once more was waste and void and darkness was upon the face of the deep. No, this was worse than original chaos, for that at least had in it the infinite possibilities of creation. But now the future is shut up in a narrow Newtonian box of known cause and predictable effect in which there is no room for miracle and nothing can happen which has not happened before.

'If Christ be not raised your faith is vain, has nothing in it ... But now is Christ risen from the dead and become the first-fruits of them that slept.' The walls of that stupid, stifling box of impossibility have been broken open; once again anything is possible. And into the awful meaninglessness of the silence of God a voice has rung out, 'Let there be light.' And – the first sunrise of the new creation lit up a massive stone rolled back from an empty tomb.

Can we still say that as though it were a fact of history? I believe we can. We can't *prove* that God raised Jesus from the dead. We can never *prove* that it was God who did anything. Nor can we be positive whether each particular story of the resurrection period was an actual event or a later elaboration by devout believers. Personally, I find most of them convincing. But even in my most sceptical moods I find that two basic elements in the stories stand unshakeably firm.

Something happened on the *third day*, otherwise there is no reason why that time reference should have crept into the story; for I think it unlikely that it arose in the first instance from a prediction by Jesus himself. Something happened to make those Christians celebrate the first day of the week from the very start. The opening verses of John's account of the resurrection, though it is probably the latest of the Gospels, contains a tell-tale word. Running back from the garden, Mary Magdalene tells Peter and John: 'They have taken away the Lord out of the sepulchre and *we* know not where they have laid him.' 'We'? But this Gospel tells of no one but Mary going to the tomb. That word shows that the compiler of this Gospel has made use of a much older tradition that agrees with the earlier Gospels and persists in all of them: that Mary Magdalene went with other women to visit the grave of Jesus early on that first day of the week and found the tomb empty. If this had been a myth told by the early church to lend substance to its teaching that Jesus was alive, why make women the witnesses, since women's testimony was not accepted in those days? Why such an ambiguous discovery capable of so many different explanations? And why did the enemies of the church endorse one of the other explanations but never refuted the story itself?

But an empty tomb does not give you an Easter. 'Him they saw not.' We need the second of the two solid bits of the tradition.

We find it in what is actually the earliest of all the statements about the resurrection. Almost all scholars now agree that in the year AD 55 Paul wrote his first letter to the Corinthians. Twice over in that letter he recites a bit of the Christian instruction which he had been taught, probably at the time of his conversion about three years after the death of Jesus, or else when he first visited the Jerusalem church only six years after. So what Paul repeated to the Corinthians in the fifteenth chapter of this first letter was what was being passed on by the first disciples within a few years of the events themselves. 'I delivered to you first of all that which I also received: that Christ died for our sins according to the scriptures; that he was buried, and that on the third day he rose again according to the scriptures and that he appeared, he allowed himself to be revealed to Peter, then to the twelve; after that he appeared to more than five hundred of the brothers at once' (of whom the majority are alive to this day, adds Paul). 'After that he appeared to James, then to all the apostles.' That was the list he had been taught. Some of it refers to stories that are mentioned or described in detail in the Gospels. Some of it is different from the Gospels. What comes through firmly and clearly is the fact that Jesus appeared, and a considerable number of people saw him. It was more than a vision such as Stephen's vision of Christ, which isn't included in any list. This was something which actually *happened* to the people concerned. So that Paul added his own unforgettable encounter with Jesus on the Damascus road as another example of the same sort of experience, though it was obviously different from the original series, 'like someone born after the proper time'.

'He appeared.' 'Jesus met them.' That simple truth, whatever it means and however it happened, comes through to us despite any amount of doubt and confusion. And all the hideous let-down and meaninglessness of the death and burial, the failure and forsakenness, is transformed into assurance and vindication.

Rembrandt painted light by emphasizing the shadows around it. I have shown the glory of the resurrection by imagining a world in which Jesus never rose again. Turner tried to convey the dance and dazzle of light by softening the outlines of all his solid objects and drowning them in radiance. When we meet the Risen Lord in faith and love our arguments and probings fall away and we have no words for wonder and fear and joy.

Now we can see that his radiant hopes of the coming kingdom were justified, for in him the new age has broken through. Now we can see that the Father had not abandoned his Son but was in him suffering the utmost loss to reconcile the world to himself. Now the cross shines with the divine love and forgiveness. Now the martyrs can endure even the loss of God in their moment of extremity because the promise has been made good. Now death is known to be the way into life, and this dying and rising is the very rhythm of creation. Now we know that the continuing cycle of the seasons will not run out into a final winter of despair, but is moving towards an eternal springtime.

PART TWO

Living in His Kingdom

This is the visitor who came to stay,
this city the kingdom he will not surrender.
Cut through the cords of your own cowardice,
then out once more with him, if eyes can bear
the blinding sunlight of the third morning;
take up the quarrel of his undying truth
in the give and take of the streets, the cut and thrust
of this tempestuous marriage of earth and heaven
which human will can never put asunder.

15

An Open Door

Look, I have set before you an open door which no one can shut.
(Revelation 3.8)

These are the words spoken to the church, spoken to the community whose strength is small, by the one who was dead and is alive for evermore and who holds the keys of death and death's domain. 'Look, I have set before you an open door which no one can shut.'

During the weeks after Easter the eyes of millions turn to a rough-hewn doorway that leads into an empty cave. Rolled back to one side is the massive stone that was meant to bar the way and make the grave impregnably final. Now that door is forever open.

Yet not far away, somewhere among the network of narrow streets in the city, on that first Easter Day there was a house of fear, a house where the door was locked. It is the hiding-place of men and women who have gone to ground until the immediate danger has passed. Like the ringleaders of Solidarity after the imposition of martial law in Poland, they are lying up to see what happens next. If you had been watching that house you might have seen some furtive comings and goings: someone slipping out for groceries; a messenger anxious to let relatives know they are safe; a frantic woman beating at the door with news; two men emerging to run into the dawning light. And every time you would have heard the wooden bar secured again behind them, making fast the door.

Being 'locked in' is the human condition of a vast number of people. Some are prisoners of poverty or oppression, walled in by denial of opportunity. Some are locked into a relationship of fear and anger that paralyses them. Sickness or disablement can be a lifelong captivity. Depression confronts its victims with high blank walls in which not even a locked door appears. Many are caught in a situation so strangely tangled that they can see no way out.

'No way out' is the heraldic motto of death's domain. Being locked in is a state of death; it is an anticipation of the tomb. So, wherever we see human beings trapped, inhibited, hemmed in, we must say with the apostle Paul, 'Death reigns.' Death reigned in that locked house where the disciples were concealed. Death's victory over them was total. And then, as Luke says in the last chapter of his Gospel: 'As they were talking about all this, there he was, standing among them.' There he was, Jesus, that most glorious Lord of life. And his familiar presence in their midst said more plainly than any words: 'Look, I have set before you an open door.' If the gates of death itself have been unbarred, there are no more locked doors of any kind. Whatever your imprisonment, and however locked in you feel yourself to be, you must believe this: *the door is open*.

I want very briefly to apply this Easter truth in three particulars.

First, it gives us the key to forgiveness. Forgiveness means absorbing the pain of a wrong instead of passing it on. But it meant more than that for Jesus. In him forgiveness means keeping the doors of communication open at all costs to yourself. Faced with hostility, Jesus never withdrew into himself, never took comfort in that last resort of pride, 'I will never speak to him again.' Like Steve Biko before the South African police, and like many Christian leaders confronting their oppressors today, Jesus insisted on meeting his judges and accusers humanly, as man to man. When Caiaphas insinuates that he has been teaching subversion to his disciples secretly Jesus replies: 'I have spoken openly to all the world. I have said nothing in secret. Ask my hearers what I told them.' That is the answer of a real communication; nothing sullen or cringing there, but an open invitation to talk. So immediately one of the guards struck him across the face. 'Is that the way to answer the High Priest?' Not the usual way, for sure. But still Jesus will not fall into the easier role of victim. 'If I spoke amiss, state it in evidence, but why strike me if I spoke well?' Forgiveness is keeping the door of a truly human communication open whatever the cost. 'Come now, let us reason together, says the Lord. Though your sins are scarlet, they may become white as snow; though they are dyed crimson, they may yet be like wool.' 'Look, I have set before you an open door – open and accessible, whatever you do to me.'

The second application of this Easter image of the open door concerns our exclusions of one another. 'Thou hast opened the kingdom of heaven to all who believe' – to the prodigal and the publican, to the disreputable, the heretical, the foreigner. The defiant inclusiveness of Jesus lived on in the church which threw open its doors to the Gentiles in spite of all that had been taught in the older religion. His people could not take it then and we cannot really take it even now. For the purity of the church we set up our check-points at the open door and demand passports of legitimacy. If the church does it, can we censure our society for doing it to people of a different colour or culture? Yet all these closed doors have the smell of death upon them, and Christ still stands among us, saying, 'Look, I have set before you an open door which no one can shut.'

Already we are looking at the third application of these words. For we are talking about institutions and systems, of which the church is one, and the nation another. There are many others – the legal system, our parliamentary system, our educational system, our business corporations, our cities, the media, the unions, the armed forces. They are necessary for the conservation and communication of certain knowledge and energies. They are necessary to us and they dictate very many of our ideas and responses. The New Testament calls these systems and institutions 'thrones, principalities and powers'. And it is by them, very often, that we find ourselves 'locked in'.

If you look carefully into many of our suicidal industrial disputes you will find as often as not that everyone concerned is a prisoner of the past, taking up a posture that is dictated not by their own judgement, nor by the real relationships they normally have with one another, but by the code of the system itself. They behave like people playing caricature parts in a melodrama.

And don't we know in our very bones that this is what is happening when we become caught in the rapids of a state of war. We are suddenly locked into a scenario of strident exaggeration and unreality, terrifyingly inappropriate to the present day, the script of which is dictated by the institution called 'national sovereignty', and there appears to be no way out.

But Easter affirms that we are not locked in, neither in our private captivities, nor our interpersonal tangles, nor as automata playing our parts in a system. There is a way out, just as there was for the Israelites trapped on the shore of the Red Sea with the cavalry of Egypt closing in behind them. The Lord who rolled back the waters of that sea, and who rolled back the stone from that tomb, has not destined us to be the prisoners of death's domain. Christ recalls us to quietness and newness of life and the freedom to go forward into a responsible relationship with our inner selves and with others.

'Look, I have set before you an open door which no one can shut.'

16

When You Can't Believe,
Make-Believe

'Seeing' is a word that rings through all the resurrection stories. 'He was seen by Cephas', wrote Paul, 'and then by the Twelve, and then by 500 brethren all at once.' Again, according to John, the disciple that came first to the tomb saw the grave-clothes and believed. Mary Magdalene turned and saw Jesus standing there, and after recognizing him, she ran and told the others, 'I have seen the Lord!' Luke's Gospel recounts how the two disciples welcomed the stranger to their home at Emmaus, where their eyes were opened and they recognized him. It was all a matter of seeing. But ever since those 40 days we have been asked to believe without the evidence of our eyes. Believing in that long-ago resurrection is difficult. Believing that it has made any great difference is harder still, whether one looks at the world, or the church, or at one's own life.

So what are we to do when our ability to believe that Jesus is actually a living reality today ebbs away, or when the very idea of any sort of relationship with an unknowable God seems merely fanciful?

At those times the first and most necessary step we can take is to admit our true state of mind, our lack of belief, and stop being ashamed or afraid of it. Jesus could apparently accept the man who said, 'Lord I believe; help my unbelief.'

And the next step is to realize that that man was not contradicting himself when he talked about belief and unbelief. You can actually believe while not believing. I mean you can act your belief while your mind disbelieves. The Gospel of John is very much concerned with the nature of belief and it reports these words of Jesus: 'Anyone who has the will to do the will of God will recognize the nature of the teaching, whether it is God-given or not.' In other words we have to act as though it was true before we can become convinced of its truth. We must put it into action in order to believe it.

That becomes more obvious if we remember that our word 'believe' meant originally 'to live by'. To live by the reality of God, even when we feel we can't grasp it; to live by the reality of God's love when we don't feel it, even when our intellects doubt it; to live by the resurrection of Jesus, even when our minds wonder whether it can be true – it is all a matter of choice, of commitment, of will. The world may call it wishful thinking; and there will be times when all we can say is: 'I'd rather live my life as though a loving God were a reality, even if I find at the end that I was wrong, than spin out my days in a godless universe. I'd rather share the illusions of Jesus of Nazareth than be a wiser man than he in any other kind of world.' But, in fact, those who hold on to the doing, the living of the faith, even when the thinking deserts them, do find in time that their recognition of its truth is restored and returns stronger and clearer than before.

You might put it in a nutshell and say, 'When you can't believe, make-believe.' Live as though it were true.

C. S. Lewis, in his great series of radio talks, loved to convince his audience that there was more truth in the old myths and fairy-tales than they supposed. He reminded them once of the story of Beauty and the Beast. She had to marry a monster. She kissed it as if it were a man. And much to her relief it really turned into a man, and all went well. Lewis also retold the tale of the unpleasant character who chose to wear a mask that made him look much nicer than he really was. And because everyone treated him as the admirable fellow he seemed to be, his personality slowly grew to resemble the mask. What had begun as a disguise had become a reality. Whenever we say the 'Our Father', said Lewis, we are pretending to be Christ, we are pretending to be the Son of God. And all the time Christ, the true Son of God, is at our side, turning the pretence into less of a pretence, more of a reality. So with that picture in mind we can begin to understand rather better what Paul was after when he wrote about us 'putting on Christ' or about Christ being 'formed in us'.

Jesus too, in his proclamation of the kingdom of God, also invited his followers to join him in a game of make-believe. God's rule over his world, he said, is very close by: you could almost reach out and touch it although it hasn't quite arrived. Then why not live as though it were already here? Why not take it by force and have it today? And in every generation since then there have been some, his happy few, who have dared to play the game of make-believe with him. Fear not, little flock, it is your Father's delight to give you the kingdom.

So let us choose to find again the magic in that little phrase 'as if'. The letter to the Hebrews, speaking of the leadership of Moses, says, 'He endured as if seeing the invisible, the unseeable.' Blessed are those who have not seen and yet have believed, have lived *as if* the unseeable were there visibly at their side.

17

From Evening to Morning

There were once two friends who were planning to spend a week away in the country. They found there were three trains in the day: one in the early morning; one mid-morning, arriving in the afternoon; and the last train that got in about 10 o'clock at night. One of them was all for catching the early train when there would be fewer people and they could arrive in time for lunch. But the other friend, who was a writer, said: 'No, let's arrive in the dark when we can't see beyond the black hedges. Let's grope our way up the lane and find the cottage gate by the scent of the honeysuckle. After a sleepy welcome and a hot drink, we'll climb to our room by candle-light and fall into bed and hear nothing but the silence around us. Then when we've slept and the first light wakes us, we can lean out under the eaves and watch the new world being made and learn the shape of the hills and greet the early birds and hold our breath for the arrival of the sun. But first we must start in the darkness.'

I think he was right. That is how everything begins, everything of real value.

> In the beginning the earth was waste and void and darkness was upon the face of the deep; and the spirit of God hovered over the face of the waters. And God said, Let there be light, and there was light, and God saw that the light was good. And God separated light from darkness; he called the light Day and the darkness Night. Evening came and morning came, the first day.

'Evening came and morning came, the first day.' That is the true measure of a day, and in most parts of the world, unlike us, people know that a day starts at nightfall. Before there can be any sunrise you must pass through the dark. Before you can be anything, you must become nothing. In order to break through into any kind of new life,

you must know the loss of the old life. That is the secret of the
Christian faith, and the Bible sets it down in its opening paragraph.
'Evening came and morning came, the first day.'

That is how the life of each one of us began. It started with a
dreadful ending. In our mother's womb the darkness was safe and
warm, and to be united with her life was the only life we knew. Then
came a rending separation and rejection that must have felt exactly
like a death. No wonder the little face was contorted with fear. No
wonder we screamed. Yet that baby's yell is a great 'Yes' to life. What
felt like death was birth. We actually died into life of a new kind, a
new dimension.

I believe each one of us carries the memory of that violent dying-
into-life throughout our days. Sometimes it haunts us as a great fear of
death. We know we are going to die again. At other times it lifts us up
with a strong conviction that we are made for life and that every death
is, like that first one, a new birth. Sometimes the death of a friend, the
death of a parent, of a husband or wife, above all the death of a child,
feels like an absolute end, a total darkness, a complete loss. At other
times we are given much more positive feelings, and although our
personal bereavement pain is still there, we are sure that for them it
has been an entry into a new dimension of life and that they are
travelling on.

Our common experiences of joy and sadness, of change and loss,
teach us again and again that the positive feelings are the truth and that
dying really does lead into new life.

When a little child goes off to school for the first time the young
mother and father may cry as though they had lost their son or
daughter, and in a way they have. Something precious has died. Yet
they know it must die if their baby is to grow up. If they hang on to
those baby days, the child will never take hold of the new life that is
waiting.

Nine or ten years later, when the child leaves school for the last
time, he or she will feel that something has died, been lost for ever.
But it must be left behind because a wider world awaits. Even our
celebrations – a twenty-first birthday, a wedding, a change of job –
contain pain as well as congratulations because something is being
lost. When a family moves home, when a person retires, when
someone loses a limb, or sight, or hearing, and always when we are
bereaved, we face another crisis of separation. We have to die a certain
death to the old if a resurrection to the new is to be found.

The final death of our own bodies, which must come to us all sooner or later, is not some unique event, but only the final loss to which all our other daily deaths lead up. We can practise dying by letting things go and accepting the loss each time for the sake of the greater maturity and richness that lies beyond it. So we may come to our final loss having formed a habit of dying into new life, with confidence that the way has always opened up into something better and will do so again. It isn't death that matters, but the hope you bring to it.

I don't want to make it sound easy or painless. It isn't. Letting the precious thing or the loved person slip through your fingers is desperately difficult, and believing that the dark will not have the last word is often more than we can manage.

Dr Cicely Saunders, of the famous St Christopher's Hospice, has told of a young model, suffering from terminal cancer, who was admitted as a patient. Her personal courage took the form of defiance towards any expression of the Christian faith which underlies and inspires the work of that hospice. But every day she flaunted the exaggerated make-up of her profession like a banner of pride. One evening towards the end she asked the nurse who was attending to her:

'Do you really believe all this?'

'All what?'

'That there's a God: that you don't just snuff out.'

'Yes, I really believe that's true.'

There followed a long silence, and then she asked,

'Do you think it's enough if one just hopes it's true?'

'I'm sure it's enough.'

A few hours later, before settling for the night, she took off her artificial eyelashes as usual, put them in their little box and handed it to the nurse saying, 'I guess I shan't need these any more.' She lived for a few more days of great peace, and when she lay dead they said she looked absolutely lovely. It isn't death that matters, but the hope you bring to it.

Why is it that Christian faith should be of special help?

First, because Jesus knows all about the darkness and is to be found there in the dark. In the dark he offers no answers. There are no answers. He brings no easy explanations, but his presence takes away the meaninglessness of the suffering. The mid-twentieth-century poet Thomas Blackburn has put this very beautifully in a poem that describes how he and his wife discovered a broken crucifix in the Alps and brought back the worm-eaten figure to hang in their home.

> Because it says nothing reasonable
> It explains nothing away,
> And just by gazing into darkness
> Is able to mean more than words can say.

'Yea, though I walk through the valley of the shadow of death I will fear no evil, for thou art with me.'

A second reason why trust in Jesus helps is that he himself followed the pattern of the evening and the morning. It was in the evening hour that his broken body was lowered from the cross and laid in the grave. And it was very early in the morning, while it was still dark, before the sun had risen, that he was once again alive and free. Those who came as mourners to the burial garden were able to watch a new world being made, learn the shape of the hills, greet the early birds and hold their breath for the arrival of the sun. For them, and for us, that is the guarantee that death is birth. Evening comes and morning comes – the first day!

18

Responding to the Divine Love

*You must love the Lord your God with all your heart, and with all your soul,
and with all your strength, and with all your mind; and your neighbour as
yourself. (Luke 10.27)*

But is God lovable?

I mean, does it make sense to talk about loving whatever we mean
by 'God'?

It's hard enough to love our neighbours, but they are at least the
same kind of beings as ourselves, capable of responding to us in all of
the ways in which we can respond to them, with liking or irritation,
trust or fear.

But does God react as we do? God is not 'as ourselves'.

Forget the cosy intimacy of our hymns. Remember those photo-
graphs of the birth of galaxies that may no longer be there for all we
know, so many billions of years has it taken the light of those events to
reach this district of the universe, since space, as Einstein might have
said, is all a matter of time. Whatever mystery it is that underlies those
unimaginably distant events – call it mind or life-force or potentiality
of being, or 'God', if that word comes naturally to you – can it be
anything but indifferent to our existence? And indifference is the true
opposite of love. It precludes relationship. It belongs to the realm of
'It', not 'Thou'.

But hold on a minute. We who *are* capable of love are of the same
stuff as those vast impersonal masses. Mere distance does not
disinherit us. Everything in the universe, it seems, however far apart,
consists of the same fundamental elements as our small planet. Every
molecule of iron in your bloodstream originated in the fusion of
elements in the heart of a star. Then if we who are star-dust can
respond with mingled awe and delight to the night sky, it would

appear that we are bilingual and need both the language of 'It' and the language of 'Thou' if we are to convey the whole truth of our human consciousness of reality.

This was the dominant insight of the Jewish philosopher Martin Buber in the first half of this century. Our experience of all that exists around us, he said, is twofold. Things and other beings may remain as inert objects of our perception, essentially common to us all, and that state of affairs is necessary to our life. On the other hand, what is out there may at times come out to meet us unsummoned, as a subject making itself known. At such moments music, which is still nothing but sound-waves impinging on our nerve ends, becomes more than a pleasant sound; it speaks, it overwhelms, it takes possession. Or a landscape ceases to be a familiar view and presents itself to us like a revelation. Or the truth which has lain concealed in a tangle of equations, eluding us for years, suddenly steps out, giving itself in its brilliant simplicity. Buber noted that this way of knowing what is there is invariably so personal to you that you are alone with it and can tell it to others only in the totally inadequate language of 'It', as a *fact*. But to you it remains a 'Thou' experience of wondering delight and gratitude. That undiluted delight and unconditional gratitude is true love for God. It was G. K. Chesterton who said: 'The worst moments for an atheist are when his heart is brimming with gratitude and he has no one to thank.'

There are other aspects of love, of course. Love is longing. Love is compassion, forgiveness, service. But, because it is the most truly mutual form of love, it is best to start with delight when thinking about God's love for us and ours for God and for our neighbour.

The Bible opens with a poem of God's delight in the successive stages of creation. Not only does God call each new stage into being, but immediately delights in its goodness. Seven times the divine pleasure is affirmed. In fact, wherever the creation is mentioned in the Old Testament God's joy in it is recalled. The same is true of God's relation to his people: 'The Lord your God is in your midst like a warrior keeping you safe. He will rejoice over you and be glad.' The same note of divine joy at the core of God's love rings through the Gospels also. 'Rejoice with me for I have found the one that was lost.' 'It is your Father's good pleasure to give you the kingdom.'

If we are to respond to the love of God with spontaneous ardour, we must let this simple truth sink in, that the mystery underlying all things, the source of existence itself, desires your presence and mine in the scheme of things unconditionally, as parents delight in their children. God wants you to *be*, more than God wants you to be good, since that is the nature of love.

So look again, if you will, into the night sky. See the unthinkable dimensions of darkness separating those incandescent masses as an 'It' – for so it is – and you will still find only indifference. There is nothing new in that conclusion. You could say with the writer of Psalm 8: 'When I consider thy heavens, what is man that thou art mindful of him?' Then recall how the unutterable beauty of things, and the intimations of meaning they convey, have from time to time come out to meet *you*, speaking at a depth no human words can reach.

And if your memories of such encounters are too sparse – for children repress them when they find the adult world avoids all mention of them – then trust the testimony of the sages, the prophets and the saints of every faith, those who were more open and perceptive than most, that they loved God because he first loved them. Trust the testimony of Jesus who demonstrated the passionate self-giving of God in a human life, and who gave us the central ritual of the eucharist as a symbol of the exchange it demands from us: take this, the divine love, and know that you matter to God. Respond with your human love, and acknowledge that he matters to you. Be aware of those around you who matter to God no less. And so love the Lord your God with all your heart and your neighbour as yourself.

19

The Greater Reality

On his way back, as he approached the house, he heard music and dancing.
(Luke 15.25)

The words come from one of the best-known stories in the world, the parable of the Prodigal Son. That house, with its ready welcome to a ne'er-do-well lad, is a symbol of God's unconditional acceptance of every human being who turns to him in whatever way. And it is significant that in Jesus's choice of imagery – for he was a consummate story-teller – the home-coming should be celebrated with the sounds of music. No doubt it wasn't the refined and formal strains of a Renaissance ensemble, nor of such instruments as those depicted in the carvings found in our mediaeval churches and cathedrals, but a primitive skirl of flutes and thump of drums, feet pounding to plaintive Jewish dance-chant. But, however it sounded, what made the music of this story remarkable was that it had not been heard in that house for a long time past. It was the home-coming of a vanished child that had revived it. Music is associated with a human being's return to God.

I have often asked myself why it is that, as fewer people feel genuinely at home in the routine of formal religion – its worship, its beliefs, its moral code – more and more, on the other hand, should find an alternative in great music. Their annual attendance at a performance of Bach's St Matthew Passion is, for a lot of people, the most religious observance of their year, even though they may be unable to subscribe to the details of the belief which inspired it. For others a symphony concert or string quartet recital with no overtly religious content may be something very close to spiritual experience. I have read a student's personal recollection of listening alone in his lodgings to a recording of Sibelius' Violin Concerto and rising from his bed afterwards to look out of the window at a world momentarily transfigured.

Is the more inarticulate, intuitive response that we make to great music at all comparable with the affirmations of the believer? Carefully researched surveys have shown that almost half the adult population of Britain has known some experience of transcendent reality which changed their understanding of life; yet they don't talk about God, because they don't have the words. The language of the churches seems too cut-and-dried and too assertive to describe their more undefined encounters with spiritual reality, and they feel that their continuing agnosticism in regard to many questions must make them unacceptable to those who are religiously convinced.

So music – and as a churchman I say this sadly – offers such folk a more accessible home to their spirits, and affirms their most private moments of vision, without raising barriers or checking their credentials. Music, in other words, is rather more like the unquestioning welcome of the father in Jesus' story, who demanded nothing else but the desire to return and be accepted. That is pure forgiveness, and, though it may seem a strange idea, that is the word the poet W. H. Auden associated with the effect of music. Comparing music with the other arts, he wrote:

> Only your song is an absolute gift ...
>
> You alone, alone, O imaginary song,
> Are unable to say an existence is wrong,
> And pour out your forgiveness like a wine.[1]

Another factor which makes music seem more inclusive in its appeal to the human spirit is that the language in which it speaks does so without words. Words are the supreme communicators, but in our civilization there are too many of them. We are tired of them and suspicious of them. Their magic is too easily manipulated. We have been let down by words, or trapped by them into some false position or other. So we prefer to leave our most private and profound experiences unspoken, lest by trying to put them into words we turn them into stereotypes that don't have the same meaning. And in every

[1] W. H. Auden, 'The Composer', *Collected Shorter Poems 1930–1944*, Faber 1950, pp. 21f.

human life those moments which help us to find a *meaning* in things are too precious to be exchanged for any inauthentic interpretation.

For meaninglessness is the worst horror that haunts this materialist society. The offer of banal, wordy meanings is almost as bad. Music does not have the words with which to provide explanations, but it does in its own language give us an assurance that there is meaning and pattern and worth to our existence. For music presents to us the dynamics of this existence, saying, as it were, 'This is the truth of how things are, this interplay of light and shadow, height and depth, enclosure and freedom, order and chaos; these exchanges of question and answer, gravity and laughter, conflict and resolution, suspense and fulfilment. This is the nature of things, and you can trust it.'

This strange capacity in music to instil a sense of pattern and significance into life makes it specially apt for bringing out the meaning of an occasion. 'On his way back, as he approached the house, he heard music . . .' It was, as I've said, a long time since those sounds had been heard in that home. There was no missing the exuberant joy of whatever was being celebrated, and the surprise of it startled the man as he came within earshot. The music drew him towards the door, though he was not sure he was going to like the explanation of it when it came. For he was the sourpuss elder brother in the story, back late from his dutiful work on the farm. One can't help sympathizing with him at that moment. He had never shared his father's softness towards the selfish younger son, yet on his account their home had become a sad place with no more parties for him. This sudden celebration was more than he could take. Even though the father comes to the door to urge him inside, the story leaves him there, undecided.

And that is the point. Music, with its extraordinary power of convincing us of a meaning and a reality beyond the sound-waves of which it consists and the sensuous pleasure it provides is a supreme go-between. It brings us to a threshold. Like Dante's spirit-guide Virgil, music can lead us to the entrance of Paradise. It is a pointer into the ultimate truth, confirming what our hearts know to be true. As in Jesus's story, the music which pours from the father's home can draw you to the very door, but then it is your will that must step across the threshold; it is your faith that must say 'Yes' to the welcome and forgiveness which the music is celebrating.

There comes a point in our response to music or art when it demands our commitment and total participation in the meaning, the values, the vision that it is communicating. If we choose then to distance ourselves in detached attention, it will take us no further. Perhaps this is why the story-teller said, 'he heard music and dancing'. For dancing means letting the music move more than your thoughts. Dancing means participating; it means entering in.

Beauty in art or in nature calls to us in a vast variety of forms. What they have in common is that the beauty draws us towards a reality beyond itself which is the source and meaning of all beauty. The philosopher C. E. M. Joad, while still a rationalist agnostic, described the impact of great music in these readily recognizable terms: 'The musical experience is not adequately described as merely a succession of feelings; it is also a kind of knowledge, and the knowledge that it conveys comes to one with the assurance of a conviction.'

A much greater philosopher than Joad, St Augustine of Hippo, writing in the fifth century, bitterly regretted the wasted years in which he had hesitated, as it were, in the dark courtyard alone, drawn by the music yet unable to commit himself to the greater reality of which it spoke that was waiting to welcome him across the threshold. This was his prayer after he had committed himself at last.

> Late have I loved thee, thou who art Beauty itself, ancient of days yet ever new. Too late have I loved thee! For, behold, thou wert within and I abroad. And there I searched for thee, I deformed, plunging among those lovely forms which were of thy making. Thou wert with me, but I was not with thee. Things, which could not exist except in thee, held me far away from thee. Thou hast called and shouted and broken through my deafness; thou hast flashed and shone and scattered my blindness. Thou hast touched me, and I burned for thy peace. When I shall hold thee fast with my whole self I shall nowhere have sorrow or stress, and my life shall be wholly alive, being wholly filled with thee.[2]

---

[2] *Confessions*, Book X, xxvii (38).

20

What Do These Things Mean?

Pleasing sounds, infectious rhythm, works of art – things enjoyable in themselves. Why look for a meaning? Why, for that matter, should anything mean something? Give a cat a bowl of food and she doesn't ask what you mean by it. And no doubt the bats in the belfry of York Minster, when they smelt smoke the other day and found things getting too hot, did not stay to argue whether it was a judgement from heaven. Fire is fire, and food is food, and sound-waves are sound-waves, and only human creatures have this itch to demand: 'What does it mean?'

It is necessary sometimes to think about this strange capacity of ours not to take things at their face value or their cash value. Of course it is not active all the time; if it were we should be mentally ill. It is a symptom of schizophrenia to be finding messages in every phenomenon. But most of us suffer from the other extreme of unawareness, blind to all significance.

The American theologian Paul van Buren once wrote: 'Some men are *struck* by the ordinary, whereas most find it merely ordinary ... The sort of speech and the sort of silence that marks off the deep ones from the superficial appears within the context of a sense of wonder, awe and joy before what is there for all to behold.'

It is there. That is the point. It is there and meaning lies within it. It is too easy, too superficial, to suppose that things are just things and that we read our meanings into them or impose our symbolic sense upon them. Things are more mysterious than that, and any artist knows that he is about the business of perceiving the significance that lies within them and trying to make it visible. In doing this he discloses more of the meaning of the very substances that he is using – the stone, the sound-waves, the syllables or the blobs of oil-paint. These are not just the incidental instruments that he uses to reveal

significance in a landscape or a musical theme. A painting is not only
about its subject but also about the interplay of colours and form. So
in such activity the artist, whether or not religious terminology comes
naturally to him or her, is being moved by the Spirit, by God.

The German woodcarver Ernst Barlach wrote in a letter to a
friend: 'Creation has no end. Ultimately the creator and the creature
are one. This force in us is the force of God, in everything – all our
labours, our longings, our struggles, our hopes, our achievements, our
joys and our angers. Art and music sometimes give us a glimpse of
undiscovered worlds.'

The sculptress Barbara Hepworth also wrote in the same vein
about the inner force in simple physical objects which I have termed
'the meaning'. 'Power', she says, 'is not manpower or physical
capacity. It is an inner force or energy. Vitality is not a physical
organic attribute of sculpture, it is a spiritual inner life.'

Or, as Jesus, who knew about the meaning of bread and wine and
water and earth and seeds, put it: 'The flesh profiteth nothing; it is the
Spirit that gives life.'

But seeing and conveying the significance of a thing is not the same
as explaining or interpreting. When the disciples asked Jesus to give
them the meaning of one of his parables, he did his best, but the
power of the original story was no longer in the explanation. How can
you put into any other words the meaning of *King Lear* or
Beethoven's last quartets? No wonder all our explanations of the
eucharist have reduced it, sometimes to absurdity. And just as
ineffectual is all the theology in which people have tried to explain
how God's own meaning has been for ever contained in a single,
particular, totally human life and death.

At their best musicians, poets, artists and good craftsmen bring
their deeper awareness and keener sensitivity to help us to exercise
what is our essentially human capacity, in a phrase of Shakespeare's
Lear, to 'take upon us the mystery of things as if we were God's spies'.

But the mystery of things is not mystical, nor is their latent
significance something that can be spiritualized away from their
honest physical reality. The meaning of bread cannot be far removed
from the dusty scent of garnered grain, the texture of heavy sacks, the
flour-powdered boards, chalk-marks on the door, the heavy wheel
and the millrace outside. So the beauty of music and poetry is bound
up with the sound-waves and the mathematics of overtones and
harmonics, with the echoes and associations and roots of the words

that make a poem. And it is the very vulnerability of all physical things that offers the space in which the divine truth and humility can operate. John Masefield wrote:

> Life's battle is a conquest for the strong,
> The meaning shows in the defeated thing.

This is the truth that is given to us to be rediscovered in every eucharist. In the smallness, the threatened actuality of the Host, we find the Presence. It is bread, pure and simple, and it is filled with Christ. We receive it as his pledge that he who fills the bread also fills the universe in each particular, physical part and is the meaning hidden within everything, awaiting our recognition.

21

Seeing Visions and Dreaming Dreams

*In their astonishment they exclaimed, 'How is it that we hear it, each one of us,
in our own mother tongue?' But others, mocking, said, 'They are filled with new
wine.' (Acts 2.12–13)*

There is a similarity between that public reaction to the great events
of Pentecost and the way in which people in every age have reacted
to the work of the artists and musicians of their own day. Wonder at
recognizing the universal language of truly inspired music and art, or
contemptuous dismissal of what seems like the latest arty intoxica-
tion. And then comes the opinion of one who sees it in more
transcendental terms.

'But Peter, raising his voice, said, "These people are not drunk, as
you suppose. No, this is what the prophet Joel foretold. God declares:
'I will pour out on everyone a portion of my Spirit, and your young
people shall see visions and your old folk shall dream dreams.'"'

To take those words about God's gift of his Spirit and apply them
to the so-called inspirations of painters, composers and poets is to
adopt a very lofty view of the arts, which some would call a falsely
romantic one. Can it be justified?

I could quote examples from the Bible which attribute the
creativity of musicians and artists to the power of the Spirit of God.
But I prefer to consider what we mean when we talk of art or music
speaking to us in a universal language. Isn't the wordless communication of a great painting or symphony, when we respond to it,
somewhat like an illumination from beyond ourselves, beyond even
the artist or composer who has seen it and expressed it?

In a favourite passage of one of my favourite books Bernard Levin has written: 'The artist – the real artist – is not painting a milk jug, or sunflowers, or the crucifixion. He is painting truth.'[1] Elsewhere in the same book he claims that the ultimate wonder of all Shakespeare's work is that it is *true*. And he writes of music in the same way. What does he mean? The wordless vocabulary of music and painting consists essentially of pattern, movement, repetition and contrast. And, if I understand him aright, what Levin means is that the truly great artists, composers and writers are bent on saying: This is the nature of things, this contradictory interplay of light and shadow, agitation and stillness, height and depth, suspense and fulfilment, gravity and laughter, question and answer, conflict and resolution, chaos and order. This is how things are; yet within them and beyond them there is ultimate meaning and transcendent beauty which, once glimpsed, changes everything. Quoting seven instances of great music, Levin says,

> All these and hundreds more musical examples point the way to our human understanding of our human duty, the duty to be transformed, to rise from darkness into light, to pursue the will-o'-the-wisp of integration and completeness until it turns out to be no will-o'-the-wisp but the shining sun of eternal truth.[2]

Does that sound too romantically overheated? Probably it does to the hard-pressed, hardheaded orchestral player. Yet in the concert hall there are many who find themselves seeing such visions and dreaming such dreams as Levin describes. Or are they, after all, only starting after some momentary will-o'-the-wisp? When they emerge on to the street, when they join the queue of traffic crawling home, do they agree with Macaulay that 'an acre in Middlesex is better than a principality in Utopia'?

It all depends on what you mean by Utopia. Is the vision of 'reality transformed' that the arts can sometimes evoke, or the dream of the biblical prophets of swords beaten into ploughshares and a new heaven and earth, no more than a never-never-land of wishful thinking? Is it an esoteric glimpse of some superior state of being unattainable in this world? Or was Wordsworth right to insist that we should locate our visions

---

[1] Bernard Levin, *Enthusiasms*, Jonathan Cape 1983; Coronet 1985, p. 72.
[2] Ibid., p. 196.

> Not in Utopia – subterranean fields –
> Or some secreted island, Heaven knows where!
> But in the very world, which is the world
> Of all of us – the place where, in the end,
> We find our happiness, or not at all.[3]

In that case, do our occasional inklings of a world transformed promise only some far distant future? Are they granted to us only to keep our hope alive and resolute? Or are they, rather, moments of revelation showing us the unguessed reality of things as they truly are all the time? As William Blake put it: 'If the doors of perception were cleansed, everything would appear to man as it is, infinite.'

It was Sir Thomas More who invented the name Utopia for this visionary realm, and the word means 'Nowhere'. The biblical term for it is 'the kingdom of God'. That is how Jews and Christians have summed up *their* Utopian dream, and they also have wondered whether it is to come true here or hereafter. On the whole they have been fairly positive that, when it comes, 'God's reign' must include this world and its history as well as the next. 'Thy kingdom come' is equivalent to saying, 'Thy will be done on earth *as it is* in heaven.'

The bad news is that we are still waiting for it, still hoping for the dream to come true, and this seems to be no nearer than ever it was. The good news, as Jesus Christ proclaimed it, is that God's reign is near, has always been near. It hasn't arrived, but it *is* at hand, within reach, so that anyone who is bold enough, fool enough, to believe that, can actually stretch out and grab the kingdom of God and live as though the world were already under the divine rule. Jesus did that, and paid for it – with his life. And he invited and enabled his friends to do the same. He called it 'taking the kingdom of heaven by storm'. You might say he was ahead of his time. But the crucial fact was that Jesus *acted* ahead of his time.

The Gospel of John suggests that it was his mother who unwittingly gave the hint that started him off. His baptism in the Jordan had confirmed his vocation. He came back to Galilee to proclaim the nearness of God's reign over this world. But then at a family wedding Mary whispered to him, 'They've no more wine.' She

---

[3] William Wordsworth, *The Prelude*, XI, lines 140–44.

couldn't have realized that those words echoed a thought that we know was already in his mind at that juncture. The old wine of Israel's religion had run out. The stone water-jars of their ritual observances were still firmly in place, and, as a Jew, Jesus was eager to fulfil them 'up to the brim'. But that wasn't enough to bring in the wine of God's justice and mercy and freedom. No, they have no wine.

We might paraphrase his enigmatic reply to her as: 'That's my problem, mother, not yours. And it isn't quite time yet. People are longing for the kingdom but are still not ready to live it.' But perhaps she's right. If we wait until people are ready we'll wait for ever. Someone has to anticipate the arrival of God's reign over the world and start behaving *as if* it were already a reality. So, serve the master of ceremonies such wine as he's never tasted before, and then we'll be off to live the future, God's future, now.

So the Gospels show us a Jesus who saw women, non-Jews, lepers, disreputable sinners, yes, *and* self-righteous leaders, *not* as everyone else saw them, but as he believed God sees them; a Jesus whose treatment of sabbath observance, poverty and wealth, disease, or the Temple cult ran counter to that of his society because it reflected the mind of God; a Jesus who called and enabled his friends to dare to be different and pay the price with him.

The Christian Utopia is the heavenly dream brought down to earth by a very small vanguard who think and live ahead of their time: the founders of a multi-racial school for South African children over 40 years ago; the village community of Arab and Israeli families, Jewish, Christian and Muslim, who run a school for peace half-way between Jerusalem and Tel Aviv; those inconspicuous men and women, many of them victims themselves, who are offering the sufferers from HIV/Aids their unconditional respect, support and affection. This is the kingdom, the bread of heaven come down to earth, which Jesus embodied and taught us to pray for.

'Father, your reign, your kingdom come, your will be done on earth, as it is in heaven. Give us today our ...' What? There is good evidence that the word Jesus used next means not 'daily' but 'of the coming day'. 'Give us tomorrow's bread today' – like the man in the parable who was shameless enough to pester his neighbour in the middle of the night for a loaf of bread instead of waiting for the morning. Give *us* tomorrow's bread, the bread of kingdom come, today. They are words not so much of petition as of commitment: 'We'll live God's tomorrow now.'

A short poem by R. S. Thomas says it perfectly:

> It's a long way off but inside it
> There are quite different things going on
> Festivals at which the poor man
> Is king and the consumptive is
> Healed; mirrors in which the blind look
> At themselves and love looks at them
> Back; and industry is for mending
> The bent bones and the minds fractured
> By life. It's a long way off; but to get
> There takes no time and admission
> Is free, if you will purge yourself
> Of desire, and present yourself with
> Your need only, and the simple offering
> Of your faith, green as a leaf.[4]

[4] R. S. Thomas, 'The Kingdom', *Later Poems. A Selection*, Macmillan 1983, p. 35.

22

The True Kingdom

Jesus then left that place, and withdrew to the region of Tyre and Sidon.
(Matthew 15.21)

People who have a strong religious faith are naturally very disturbed when God appears to change his mind, but those are the moments which we may justly describe as a revelation. So long as our speculations and experiences endorse our fixed ideas we may speak of a tradition but not of a revelation, for revelation implies something startling and new – a discontinuity. Jesus Christ had such an intimacy with God that we might have supposed that he at least could never be taken by surprise. Yet even to his mind there were such moments of disclosure and change of direction. One of these is recorded in the fifteenth chapter of Matthew's Gospel, and it inaugurated such a reversal that Christians have hardly come to terms with it even now.

The Jewish homeland in which most of the biblical story unfolded was confined to the central mountain plateau of Palestine, the Lake of Galilee, the River Jordan and the southern desert. That was the Holy Land where God's separated people lived out their history of obedience, disobedience and spiritual discovery. The sea played no part in their story and served merely as a symbol of all that was hostile and uncontrolled. The ministry of Jesus also was entirely landlocked, and he was content to see his mission in these limited terms. 'I have been sent', he said, 'only to the lost sheep of the house of Israel', and he placed his disciples under the same restriction as a matter of course. The tenth chapter of Matthew's Gospel records him as saying: 'Go not into any of the Gentile roads and enter not into any city of the Samaritans, but go rather to the lost sheep of the house of Israel.' Salvation is of the Jews, and within that narrow countryside God's purpose is to be carried out.

But on this occasion, in order to avoid a premature conflict with the authorities, Jesus withdrew from the traditional Jewish territory and came into Lebanon, as we call it now, down to the region of the great Phoenician ports of Tyre and Sidon. For the first and only recorded time Jesus stands looking out to the level horizon of the sea. What did it say to him whose vocabulary had been wholly of corn-fields and sheepfolds, vineyards and lakeside fishing nets? Impact there must have been, for he was of all men most responsive to the visible world. His eyes were accustomed to a landscape of small plots enclosed by boundary walls; he had grown up to recognize the frontiers between one man's demesne and the next; one tribal heritage and another. His landlocked world was a network of *barriers*. But here the dark blue Mediterranean stretched without line or marker as far as the eye could see, and the galleys ploughed their paths hither and thither without thought of trespass. Even that straight horizon-line was only the limit of man's sight. And down there among the rigging and the wharves of the fortified harbour, Greeks and Romans, Syrians and Egyptians and sailors from any port between Cornwall and Ceylon, the slave and the freeman, the honest and the crook, accepted one another in the tough salty brotherhood of trade. As I read the Gospels I am convinced that the sights and smells of this foreign coastland stirred in this Jewish visitor a subversive thought that had already been forming in his mind.

Wasn't this a truer likeness to the kingdom of his Father who made each new sunrise for the good and the bad alike, and sent the rain on the unjust as well as the just? Wasn't this nearer to that openness which he himself practised as a child of that kingdom by associating with the disreputable and accepting the hospitality of sinners? And could God's reign ever be established among a people who through-out history had turned their backs on this great sea in revulsion and concentrated all their passion upon one small, holy land? He had already aroused the fury of his own village by recalling his heavenly Father's care for a woman of Sidon. He had cried to the towns of the Galilee lakeside that it would be more tolerable for Tyre and Sidon on the day of judgement than for them. And the trusting faith of a Roman officer had opened for him a vision of Gentiles streaming into God's kingdom from east and west, from north and south. Yet something compelled him still to limit his vocation to the Jewish people. Had he been right? And must he forever forbid his followers to go down any Gentile road or visit a Samaritan city?

The issue was brought to the test by that native woman accosting him in the street. Matthew makes the point by calling her a Canaanite, that ancient name for the people who were to be driven out by the Chosen Race. The disciples were asking him to send her packing. Then why did he turn to *them* with the words, 'I have been sent only to the lost sheep of the house of Israel,' unless they were spoken out of an inward struggle and perplexity? Then, as we do if we are wise, he put his problem squarely to the one who had raised it. 'It is not right to take the children's food and throw it to the dogs.' There in its full harshness is the doctrine of exclusiveness, and Jesus stated it blatantly as though challenging her to help him: 'So, what am I to do?' Back comes her answer: 'Yes, but even the dogs live on the scraps that fall from their master's table.'

O woman, daughter of Tyre, with your cheeky courage, great is your faith, for it has launched the universal, world-wide, Catholic Church! Let us never forget that you and I and virtually the whole of Christendom are the dogs. The knowledge of Christ is available to us only because of Jesus's commitment to inclusiveness, only because of his response to that moment of revelation when the God of the scriptures appeared to change his mind.

The short visit to the seaside was over. But the sea had flowed into the minds of those disciples. From now on it becomes central to biblical history. Beside that same sea, some three years later, Simon Peter had a dream or vision during the noontide siesta in which he was ordered to eat food that was taboo in his Jewish observance. How could God contradict himself in this way? It was he who had given the law that forbade such food, just as it was he who had called the Hebrew race to separate themselves socially and culturally from non-Jews. But now new freedoms are at work in the world. God is not bound. He can cleanse the unclean if he will and Peter must not gainsay him.

So off the apostle goes with the messengers to the Gentile house in Caesarea, yet another sea-port along that coast, the headquarters of the Roman procurator. Peter comes to the threshold of the centurion's home. His Jewish feet protest against the crossing. 'You know that it is contrary to our law that I, a Jew, should enter this house.' Yet in obedience to his vision he did it. And then, as he starts to answer Cornelius's question and retell something of the story of Jesus Christ, he recognizes that those untutored Gentiles are receiving the pentecostal gift of the Holy Spirit. He cannot deny the evidence of his eyes. He cannot withhold the baptism which that evidence demands. What is more, he has the courage to defend his action and to cast his vote in the synod when that eccentric local experience is being appraised for general application. The debate was raging furiously between the policies of exclusion and the policy of an open door. They were not ungenerous or uncharitable men, but they cared for truth as well as love, and they could not countenance something that was theologically impossible and ritually forbidden. They were willing to be flexible on inessentials, but could not play fast and loose with one of the definitive ordinances of their faith. 'I am the Lord your God. I have made a clear separation between you and the nations.'

But Peter had felt the sea sweeping in past the old bastions. He spoke out on behalf of revelation. God is not blocked into the past. God is never the prisoner of his own regulations. God's comings and goings are not limited even to the means of grace he himself has given. And when he does a new thing it is not for us to tell him that it is impossible. We have only to recognize what he is doing. Recognition is the special gift of the Holy Spirit. It is the way he intervenes. He works always by opening people's eyes to see what they have not seen before. This is what we ask for when we pray for the guidance of the Holy Spirit. In the coasts of Tyre and Sidon Jesus recognized the much greater thing that his Father was doing beyond the sheep of the house of Israel. In the home of Cornelius Peter recognized that God was breaking his own rules. And in the synod that day they all recognized that God had broken down the wall of partition between Jew and Gentile which had been the very buttress of their ancient faith.

It is precisely in that sense that we are being asked to recognize other confessions as true churches and their ministries as true ministries of word and sacrament. God is not asking us to bestow recognition upon one another as though we were some universities' board validating a new course. We are long past the point of checking up on each other to see whether each has got what it takes. We are being invited to open our eyes to one another with the same shock of delighted recognition which Peter experienced when he looked into the faces of Cornelius and his Gentile friends – 'God gave them no less a gift than he gave us when we put our trust in the Lord Jesus Christ.'

The time has come for all the churches to meet and know one another's congregations, and to recognize in them the same living presence of Christ, the same gospel and the same hope. We have to recognize in them the fruit of the one baptism which has brought us all into Christ. We have to recognize in their breaking of bread the same inexplicable reality of the presence of Christ and the same participation in his eternal self-offering to the Father. We have to recognize in one another's ministries the same pastoral and mediatorial gift, interpreted no more variously than it is within our own church.

But there is not the remotest chance of any mutual recognition of Christ in one another until we begin to take the simple step of attending one another's worship and learning about one another's programme of action and study. 'Welcome one another', said Paul, 'as Christ has welcomed us.' Welcome people of a different social background to your hospitality and welcome their invitations to you. Welcome other confessions as true churches in one communion in Christ. Welcome women into roles that have been considered possible for men only. Welcome the participation of workers in the planning and decision-making that only the executives have handled in the past. Welcome lay people into the decision-making and the government of a church that has hitherto left that charge in exclusively clerical hands. Welcome people of a different creed and race into the fellowship of those who struggle for spiritual values in our society.

We find it difficult. Two thousand years after Jesus first saw the sea and its significance we still prefer our fences and our little dividing walls. Two thousand years after he died for insisting upon inclusiveness, we unearth the old arguments that prove it is impossible.

Well, that is the spirit he confronted, and we shall confront it more starkly in the next few decades. In the coastlands of Tyre and Sidon Jesus had caught the vision of the open sea; but he returned to live it out for his remaining months in the narrow homeland. He understood now why his vocation was to be limited to those confines; and when the call of the Greeks, the Gentile world, came to him again, his answer was that the seed of corn must fall and die before there could be a harvest of freedom. There will be many a dying for us also if we insist upon his inclusive welcome. Many of our most cherished customs and ways of thought may have to be crucified as the price of the church's salvation and ultimate unity. But in the end, if those who are faithful persist, 'the earth shall be filled with the knowledge of the Lord as the waters cover the sea'.

23

Better Together

The Oxford University Diary for 1996 contains the entry:

February 21. Ash Wednesday. Torpids.

To those initiated into the archaic jargon of Oxford, it means that the college boats begin their four days of racing on the river on Ash Wednesday. In the summer term the river races are called Eights, and colleges enter their best crews. But in the Lent term, while the university boat is training for the race against Cambridge on the Thames in London, only the second-best crews from the colleges compete here. And because in these bitter cold days they turn out sometimes looking and feeling like creatures just emerged from hibernation, they have been scornfully named the Torpids, or sluggish ones.

The river in Oxford is too narrow for boats to race abreast. They compete in single file, each trying to bump the one ahead. Those crews who succeeded in this on one or more of the four days and finished the week in a higher position up the line than they had been would certainly have been celebrating, while those who are now in a lower place would have been drowning their sorrows. So at the end of the week a fair number of rowing men and women may be regretting their disregard of the spirit of Ash Wednesday – if they have any idea what that scrap of ecclesiastical jargon stands for.

'Ash Wednesday. Torpids.' We who know what the first of these means and would like to take good advantage of Lent might learn a thing or two from the college crews, even if some of them may be a bit torpid at this moment. For the past weeks, those crews have been undergoing what are called the Trials, the final testing out of more than the eight that are required in the boat, in order to pick the best of them for the actual races. The Trials, they are called, and that is exactly the meaning of the word 'temptation'. Jesus was going through his trials in the wilderness before he was finally picked to be our representative and our champion against sin.

If you were down at the river last week, what you would have seen was a glorious level of fitness and stamina and control, the result of weeks, in fact two terms, of steady rehearsal and practice. For to gain that control and that stamina, ever since October those men and those women have been under the most rigid discipline. That musty, old-fashioned word is strangely embraced by their youthful enjoyment. We think of it as a negative, restrictive idea. Discipline? Sounds a bit last-century. And yet they have freely surrendered their spare time to the tyranny of a rowing coach demanding extraordinary exactions, sometimes very painful, but they have accepted that discipline. And indeed it has always been so. Even the apostle Paul used the example of sportsmen in training. 'Every athlete learns self-denial', he says in the first letter to the Corinthians, 'and I bruise my body and bring it under control.'

But the crew of a racing eight needs an additional discipline beyond that of a runner or a tennis champion. Those individual men and women, each at the top of their form, must learn to respond like a single body, each one totally obedient to the command and the combined action and the shared mind of the crew as a whole. In rowing there are no stars, as there are in athletics or tennis. There is no 'man of the match', as in football or even cricket. Together the crew and the coach have decided on the strategy of their race, even perhaps on some technical experiment, for rowing does not stand still. It is always moving into new ways, improving. But then the seven front rowers follow with perfect precision the rhythm set by the stroke, and the stroke is totally ruled by the cox, the smallest person in the team, very often a woman, who is the eyes and the brain of the crew throughout the race. Then, to make sure that even she is not a star, if they win the cox is thrown into the river, for there is no big shot in a racing boat.

I only once went in for this sort of racing and I am ashamed to speak of it. But I did have a similar experience long ago in Africa when I joined a fishing crew on a night expedition on Lake Victoria. No concessions were made, no special position allowed, for the only white man in that crew, as we set out as the sun went down flaming into the lake. There were a number of struts, on each of which a paddler sat, one on each side, two by two, down the length of the boat. As we went out we also had to keep in perfect time, and on and on and on it went, for we travelled for many miles along the coast. Out in the open lake the waves were as high as they would be on a sea, and I often trembled to think what would happen to our narrow canoe as we paddled on and on. After a while the muscles of my back were aching unbearably; it was like a hot iron pressed between my shoulders. But I had to keep my eyes on the young boy just ahead of me, so healthy, so fit, and inexorably on and on we went, and I could not break the rhythm.

Eventually we landed on a patch of shore in the moonlight, but the wind was too high for fishing just then, so we all huddled up together in a mass and went to sleep under our blankets. Eventually we were kicked awake by the man who was in charge, because the wind had come down and out we must get and pay out the net from the boat as it circled round and came back from further up the shore to drag the fish in. The two ends were brought together, and one by one we followed each other, pulling on that heavy rope, that wet rope, as we went up the shore. We handed our bit of rope to a young boy who was winding it together and then went back down the line and took up our place further down and again went on with the hauling. That also was very painful. At one moment as I was pulling up the slope of the sand, a man walked back in the opposite direction to take his turn again, and I saw that he was rubbing his shoulders as he went down and I said, 'We all have the same pain.' In the moonlight I saw him grin and he said, 'And the one power'.

The Roman Catholic Archbishop Derek Worlock, who died not long ago, was a wonderful partner to the Anglican Bishop David Sheppard. They had their motto there in Liverpool: 'We do it better together.' That is the absolute key word of the Christian life. It is a great mistake to present it as an individual struggle for personal salvation or holiness. Of course there are decisions which we must take for ourselves and say, 'Here I stand.' There are moments when someone has to be the first to make a breakthrough, like Peter entering the home of a Gentile and baptizing his household. But remember that at once Peter made it an issue for the whole synod to decide; he shared the decision with the rest. The cult of particular saints was foreign to the spirit of the early church; it developed out of the commemoration of the noble army of martyrs all together.

For the kingdom of God which Jesus proclaimed and took hold of is meant to be an alternative community, a counter-culture, whose members are demonstrating different values and relationships from those of the mainstream. So while it may be easier to be different all by yourself, this misses the whole point of the demonstration. We are not called to be little Christs, but to be the one body of Christ, and in that fellowship, says Paul, not one of us lives or dies as a lone performer. Whether our calling lies in a religious community or in the fellowship of other disciples who are in the same place, we do it better together. How else could we be God's alternative to the current adoration of celebrities, or the belief that the common good is best achieved through the competitive struggle of individuals each in pursuit of his own interests? That is the abomination against which we have to protest as Christians, protesting in the way we live together. For the world around us is now following the injunction that we find several times describing the situation in the days of the Judges. 'In those days there was no king in Israel, but each man did according to what seemed good in his own eyes.'

Down in the muddy sea-bed of the Lake of Galilee, they found a few years ago a boat that dates from the time of Jesus. Wonderfully preserved in the wet mud, it has now been raised and restored and is visible to visitors. They say it is typical of the larger fishing smacks that Jesus would have known. It had a square sail like an Arab dhow, but it was held together by six strong thwarts from one side to the other of the boat, with two rowers on each and a seat in the stern for the man in charge of the tiller. And that is what Jesus chose as the best device for training his followers. In Matthew's Gospel, when the twelve are named, he puts the names in pairs, the fellow rowers, as he remembered them. For they had to learn a mutual awareness and response and absolute obedience to the whole team. We know that they had a common purse. Of course they weren't spending all their time in fishing, but when they were doing the new work to which Jesus had called them, he sent them out two by two. There were to be no loners. Even that work must be shared. And it wasn't all work either. When they did plan a day off, they went together. They walked together in the fields, they went up into the hills as a group, they ate together. That was most important of all. Did you know that there are ten different meals recorded in the Gospels, an extraordinary thing for a book of spiritual guidance. The Son of Man came eating and drinking, and we have remembered him ever since simply by doing so.

So during the six weeks of Lent, how about using these weeks of discipline to put down the natural loner in myself, to cut out the first-person singular from my programme, to cultivate the plural of the kingdom of God, and to give priority to those activities that I share? So each of us may come to Passiontide and Holy Week and Easter with a clearer understanding and appreciation of the one pain and the one power.

24

The Ordinary Becoming Extraordinary

Having spent many a summer holiday in my boyhood in the Highlands of Scotland, I became accustomed to the character of some of the Presbyterian ministers who preached to us in the local church on Sundays. They were men like the Old Testament prophets for whom God was very stern, and yet with that God they had an extraordinary, simple, intimate and direct relationship. So I can believe the story that was told me about one of them who ministered to a farming community on the north-east coast. During one summer they had many, many months of drought and the fields were dry and the flocks were looking for water in vain. He called his congregation on Sunday morning to pray for rain. He exhorted them and they prayed long, and he led them in long prayer and drops began to fall. And they prayed more fervently because they needed a great deal, on and on, and they praised the Lord when the rain became heavier. But then there was an absolute cloudburst and it poured down from the roof. There was a flash of lightning and a great roar of thunder, and the minister was heard to say 'Na', Na' Lorrd, dinna be rridiculous!'

I think the disciples might have been tempted to say just that when they heard Jesus speak the words which are recorded in the sixth chapter of Luke's Gospel, which we call the Beatitudes. Because it really was absurd, wasn't it? That poverty and hunger, sorrow and victimization should be matters for congratulation? That the rich and the well-fed, the merry and the popular were people to be pitied simply because one day in the far future their roles were going to be reversed?

Well, some might have shut up at that point, but to those who were still listening he went on to even more outrageous statements.

'Offer the other cheek when somebody hits you in the face. If they snatch your cloak then take your shirt off and give it to them as well. Give to every beggar who asks, in the High Street or anywhere else. And if a visitor goes off with your favourite book or some little object that you prize, don't try to get it back.' Yes, ridiculous isn't it? But when those statements are read out in church, the congregation says: 'This is the Gospel of Christ.' I have no doubt that many people, including me, add quietly, 'Well of course he didn't mean it literally. It was a deliberate exaggeration. After all he doesn't want a following of fanatics.' And in a way we are right because his church consists of ordinary people. The blessed, the beatified, were ordinary, not supermen and superwomen. The apostle Paul addressed his letters to the saints at Ephesus, in Colossae, at Philippi and so on.

The Old Testament book of Daniel comes from the time when the holy ones of the Most High were the Jews, the chosen people. In it Daniel has an extraordinary vision, a nightmare: the ocean boiling under a hurricane, great monsters coming out of the sea. This was not literal, but it is not to be watered down either, because he was seeing a terrifying future when the Jews would be oppressed by four great empires struggling against one another for power, whose armies would pass up and down across their land. And it was then that he said, 'The holy ones of the Most High, you the chosen people of God, shall possess the kingdom for ever.' The saints are ordinary men and women facing the power of evil but doing extraordinary things; the ordinary becoming extraordinary.

After all, didn't those who can remember, as I do, the summer of 1940 hear the voice of Winston Churchill on 13 May: 'I have nothing to offer but blood, tears, toil, sweat'? And on 4 June: 'We shall defend our island whatever the cost may be. We shall fight on the beaches. We shall fight on the landing grounds. We shall fight in the fields and in the streets. We shall fight in the hills. We will never surrender.' He wasn't talking to heroes, but to very frightened people. He didn't say, 'We shall win!' He was quite realistic. And we didn't say, 'That's just rhetoric; that's deliberate exaggeration.' Churchill knew he was talking to very ordinary people, but he was calling us to be extraordinary, to go beyond the ordinary of our own nature. And so it was with Jesus. No wonder they thought he was beside himself. They thought he was crazy. But Christianity is not sensible. It is not politically correct, is not moderate or safe, or comfortable.

The Festival of All Saints is a reminder of the ordinary people who became extraordinary, and reminds us also that we who are ordinary are called to be extraordinary. So don't let us water down the hard challenge of Jesus. At first the celebration of All Saints was strictly the celebration of the martyrs, the thousands who were faithful through the years of persecution, whatever the cost. And the ten statues on the West Front of Westminster Abbey are reminders to us all, as we reach the end of this terrible century, that more Christians have been martyred in the past hundred years than in all previous history, most of them unnamed. They are specially in our minds today because they speak of the very heart of Christianity.

Dietrich Bonhoeffer, one of those ten, who was executed in 1945 for his stand against Hitler, once wrote: 'When Christ calls people, he bids them come and die.' Is that just rhetoric? Is that another of the exaggerations? No, because it can be taken in several ways. We start by dying to self. We go on to live lives that are poured out for others, and none of us knows whether we may not be called to a literal interpretation, as others have been and will be, to lay down our lives rather than deny our faith. It isn't for us to choose which of those interpretations shall be ours. It isn't for us to draw the line. We must be ready for the lot. We must begin now. So it is in keeping with being a saint to go beyond the call of duty, to dare to be a bit ridiculous, to be a little more extravagant with our patience, our forgiveness. To try something beyond the ordinary.

And what about prayer to the saints? What about calling on their help? What about miracles? It is a problem, isn't it? We have to be twentieth-century people even if we do become ridiculous. Well, I know that as I frequently lose things, I call on Saint Antony and funnily enough, again and again it does work.

Perhaps a little more seriously, I'll tell you a story of a holiday that my wife Peggy and I took in Vicenza a few years ago. I not only lose things, I lose my way. We had lost our way too much that day and we were short-tempered and we were rather hurting each other. And I knew it was my fault and didn't really want to admit it. Finally we got to a beautiful church and there on the wall was a little bronze statue that halted us. It was an image of Father Kolbe, that almost unknown Catholic priest who, when a group were called together for some offence and were all condemned to be burnt alive, and one other poor man began to weep and remember his family and his children, and pleaded for mercy, Father Kolbe stepped forward and took his place.

There before the wall of that beautiful church we stood and gazed at that little bronze figure of an emaciated man wearing bedraggled prison garb, offering himself. We went out and on our way to the station. I lost my way again, but this time there was no recrimination or any shame because we found we were elated, lifted above the ordinary. We were in the presence of the extraordinary and it made all the difference.

One final story. On our way back from Provence this summer, we got out of the train several stations too early because everybody else seemed to be getting out and we hadn't been counting the stations. So we found ourselves on a platform we didn't recognize. We turned to get back into the train but it was already moving; and we had all the arrangements ahead of us and were going to miss the lot. A delightful young porter caught up with us and he could speak a little English. He asked us the problem. He led us to the station-master who spent a quarter of an hour yelling down the telephone until finally it was all fixed. Another train was going to pick us up and take us to another station where a special train was going to be stopped for us which would take us to where we would get our underground train. We arrived safely back, only an hour and a half late.

But just as we were leaving that station I turned to the young porter who had been interpreting for us and comforting us in all our fuss. I said, 'I'd like to be able to write to you afterwards. What is your name?' 'Antoine.' Antony. Ridiculous, isn't it?

25

Fellow Citizens with the Saints

As for me, the Lord has led me in the way to the house of my master's kinsmen.
(Genesis 24.27)

These old stories of the patriarchs, Abraham, Isaac, Jacob and Joseph, are like the family legends told by the Bedouin in the deserts of Arabia and North Africa today. You must imagine a group of men and children lounging on the carpets of a broad black tent after the evening meal, the women listening from the shadows in the background, while the white-bearded head of their clan recites a tale of some famous ancestor.

> You see, [he says,] he was a wanderer like us, not one of the people of the land who were settled on their farms and their big cities. He was different, and he wanted his family to stay different from the people around them. His son was a young man now – that precious son he had waited for so long and had almost lost again. He didn't want him to marry one of the local girls and become just like everyone else. He called his steward and made him swear he'd find a wife for the boy from some other branch of the wanderer's clan. For he didn't fancy he had much longer to live himself.
>
> So the steward set out and travelled north towards the homelands of the clan, with several camels in train. For weeks they were on the move until he reckoned they must be near the old family lands. It was just at the hour for the evening prayer that he came to a well with a city wall beyond it. He tethered his camels and said his prayers, putting his cause in God's hands. 'When the girls come out to draw water, I shall ask them for a drink. Let the one who offers to water my camels as well be the girl I'm looking for.' And, sure enough, God looked after him faithfully. A lovely girl came out from the city, went down to the well and started to climb back with a full water-pot on her shoulder. The steward ran up and asked for a drink. She lowered her pot to his lips,

and when he had finished she said, 'Now I'll draw water for your camels too', and started to fill the cattle-trough. At that he dared to ask what family she belonged to and whether he and his beasts might be given lodging there. And when she told him she was a daughter of Abraham's nephew, the steward exclaimed in wonder, 'Blessed be the Lord, the God of my master Abraham, who has not failed to keep firm faith with my master. As for me, the Lord has led me in the way to the house of my master's kinsmen.'

Even in these days of go-it-alone individualism, belonging to a family, having your own people, is an immense source of comfort and identity. So we find lonely people taking a keen interest in chasing their family tree, and in fact almost everyone gets excited, or perhaps put out, on learning that a mere acquaintance is in fact a distant relation.

Unhappily, families aren't always good news. The nearest and dearest can be possessive and smothering. A family tradition may become a prison. The contempt of close relatives, or their lack of appreciation, or sheer blindness, can be utterly crippling. Jesus of Nazareth knew that. Mark tells us in chapter 3 of his Gospel that when his family heard of the crowds that mobbed him they set out to take charge of him, for people were saying, and they may themselves have said it, that he was out of his mind, demon-possessed, just as the scribes were saying. And on his return to Nazareth where he had grown up, he came to his own people and his own did not accept him. Jesus knew the potential destructiveness of a family.

But he also knew that it is not good for the human creature to be alone. Jesus did not opt for isolation. He did not become a loner. Jesus created around himself an alternative family. Twice over, Mark's Gospel emphasizes this alternative, this contrast. The family's attempt to take Jesus in charge is immediately preceded by his choice of the twelve apostles and is followed, upon the arrival of the family, by Jesus's saying of those who were sitting in that circle around him, 'Here are my mother and my brothers.' And again, three chapters later, following the disbelief of his home town, he immediately reacts by sending his new family out in pairs to share his mission.

That new family which Jesus needed, which he gathered around himself to share his task and his power, which he calls his mother and his brothers and his sisters, is what we celebrate on All Saints' Day. Through our baptism we have been born into this alternative family of Jesus Christ, and through our struggling faithfulness and his constant grace we remain his fellow heirs. You and I can say with Abraham's steward, 'As for me, the Lord has led me in the way to the house of my master's kinsmen.'

Those brothers and sisters of Jesus, the people of his clan, bear the family likeness, for they have the same spirit within them. The sign by which you can recognize them is the readiness with which their water-pot is lowered to quench your thirst or anyone else's, the cup of cold water offered in Christ's name. Only he can give the living water for the human soul, but his people are like him in pouring out their kindness to any who need it, including the camels who drink so much.

We are fellow citizens with the saints, says Paul, and more than that – members not only of the same community but of the same family, the household or lineage of God. Mary does not ask of us the homage due to a queen, but the devotion and trust we might feel for a wonderful mother. Peter does not want you to kiss his toe but as a younger brother or sister to lend a hand with the fishing. But All Saints' Day is most specially the festival for recognizing our kinship with the unnamed, unsung members of the clan whose hidden lives have borne the likeness of Jesus radiantly, and inspired others to love him. You will have your memories of such saints, whose lives have crossed your path, as I have mine, and today we acknowledge our debt to them and we thank God for making us members of such a family, with such a heritage.

I think of my grandfather, a retired colonel of the Indian army: of his lined face with its heavy moustache, etched in the light of an oil-lamp, as he prayed at my bedside after reading me a Bible story, when I stayed with him as a child. I remember an old African woman in Uganda who had been a Bible teacher for 50 years. In her tiny mud hut she had nothing but a few cloths on a straw mattress, a wooden stool, a hoe, a few utensils, and her Bible and prayer book in a basket hung on a nail. But it was to her that Peggy and I would go when we were depressed, for the sake of her delighted welcome and her perfect happiness. The face of a French woman comes to mind, one of the Little Sisters of Jesus, whom I met in Kabul in 1968. For thirteen years she had been living in the poorest suburb of the city up a steep muddy lane, earning her living in a leather-work factory alongside her Afghan neighbours, not preaching but being present as a Christian, and tending in her home, with two new Sisters recently arrived, the tiny chapel which was their powerhouse. There she and the Catholic chaplain to the Italian embassy invited me to celebrate the eucharist for them – another pitcher of water lowered to a stranger's lips. So today I commemorate Grandfather Robert and Damali of Uganda and Chantal, knowing I fall pitifully short of their Christlike sanctity, yet marvelling that they are, in Christ, my kith and kin.

But remember, this family of Jesus, this people of God, are not just exceptionally kind and gentle men and women. Even in the worst of societies people are not hated and persecuted and killed for being nice. Ever since Abraham, God's people have been strangers, different, and they strive to stay different. This is God's protest movement, this is a clan of revolutionaries. These are the ones who bear witness that the world is wrong in its values and its judgements. We are here to be a different people and to stay different in our defiance of the world's idea of power, our defiance of the world's idea of success, our defiance of the world's idea of marriage, our defiance of the world's view of death.

Just how different we are is expressed in an amusing version of the Beatitudes which I came across recently:

> Pathetic are those in any sort of need, for they are obvious failures.
> Pathetic are the sorrowful, for they embarrass the rest of us.
> Pathetic are those of a gentle spirit, for they shall be kicked around.
> Pathetic are those who hunger after justice; they are crying for the moon.
> Pathetic are the ones who show mercy; everyone will take advantage of them.
> Pathetic are those whose hearts are pure, for they miss all the fun.
> Pathetic are the peacemakers, for they shall be called wet.
> Pathetic are those who suffer persecution in the cause of right. We are sorry for them, but they set themselves against law and order.

You recognize that voice, you know we have to stand against it, as all the saints in all the ages have stood against it. And on this day, in the company of these magnificent brothers and sisters whom God has given us, we pledge ourselves again to live in defiance and in love.

26

The New People

William Golding, in his brilliantly imagined novel *The Inheritors*, takes us into the experience of a family group of the sub-human species, *Homo neanderthalensis*. Marvellously he conveys the strong affection between them, the humour and courage of their rudimentary skills, the dimly groping coherence in minds that can picture past impressions and impending events, can communicate in primitive speech and by sharing consciously the same unspoken thought, can at moments of extreme helplessness look in trembling worship toward vague material beings above the snowline, but cannot marshal these fleeting mental experiences into a consistent process of thought. Neanderthal Man was one of evolution's experiments which did not go further, for he was not a direct progenitor of *Homo sapiens*.

When the novel begins to describe the coming of the New People one realizes with a shock of dismay that this family group is doomed. First they dream of the New People and of a great change. Then they smell the New People in the forest around. First one, then another, of the family fails to return. But when a pair of them actually see the New People in their encampment they feel an innocent curiosity and fascination rather than the fear that might have saved them. They have no comparisons by which to identify and comprehend the newcomers' long domed foreheads, their alcohol or their arrows. The future that has invaded their world is incomprehensible, and they go down before it. In the final scene the individual with whom we have been most deeply involved throughout the story is suddenly distanced from us by a terrible change of pronoun. *It* scrabbles for a hold upon the floating tree trunk, the red fur between its shoulders bright in the setting sun, before the tree lurches over the brink of the waterfall.

The tragic irony of Golding's novel rests in the fact that the enormously superior intelligence of the New People is so heartlessly destructive. Is this supreme advance in evolution really a regression? But supposing our human history were to be invaded by a future in which the New People were inwardly directed by love and freedom and truth, would that not be a breakthrough worth dreaming of, worth working for?

That is exactly what the Christian message is saying. The gospel is the good news, the almost unbelievably good news that a new kind of man, and through him a new kind of world, has arrived. From the first the Christian message was an adventist proclamation. The kingdom of the future is approaching, is here. Advent is not just preparing for another Christmas, but recapturing and rethinking the fact that Christianity is an adventist faith.

It says that the real fulfilment of the history of human beings and the life of the world is being given out of the future. It is not being developed out of the past and the present. The chain of cause and effect does not stretch forward to the end. That is the impression we live with, but it is an optical illusion. The future is not going to be made by us or marred by us. It is being given by God.

But the future that is being given to us is not the spiritualized heaven of the hymns nor the Utopia of political visionaries. Like the resurrection of Jesus, it is the new creation projected into the old, the power of the future transfiguring the present. Ours is an adventist hope, but not an otherworldly one. The Risen Christ is the incarnation of the life of the future kingdom. In him men and women met the new creation in the midst of the old. Through his presence with them and in them they began to become the new people, living among the old. Now they could draw existences not out of the inheritance of the past but out of the resources of the future.

'Aforetime ye walked according to the course of this world. But God made us alive together with Christ and raised us up with him and has enthroned us with him in the heavenly places.'

But let us be more specific and say what this means in very simple terms. If the earth in its planetary orbit swung even fractionally nearer the sun it would become a different kind of world in which, if there was any sort of life, it would be quite a new life system. If human consciousness became even fractionally more conscious of God we would become a new humankind. This happened in Jesus. He was the new man because his entire beginning was in continuous response to the Father. Every breath he breathed voiced the name 'Abba'. To him the kingdom was simply the closeness of the Father. It was the realization of Emmanuel.

That is how he was so sure that the future is full of grace and open to anyone who will trust and return. The kingdom is intended for all unconditionally. Men and women have not to strive to improve themselves but only to enter by the narrow gate of accepting the fact that they are accepted.

For the kingdom is inaugurated by a death and a new beginning which draws a line between the column of all past accounts. Those who cross that line cease to be debtors; nor do we carry any credit cards into the kingdom, for if we did it would not be a new beginning.

So we are called to live in the kingdom while we still await the kingdom. The tension between the 'already here' and the 'not yet' is the mainspring that gives us our drive and momentum. We are invited to live in a relation of such closeness to God that our behaviour will begin to correspond to his nature. That is the message of the Sermon on the Mount.

In other words, we allow our certainty about the future that God is giving to throw its light upon everything in the present. The future in which all things will find fulfilment in accordance with the will and nature of God is already pressing itself into the present world to question it and change it. Those who are living in the light of the coming kingdom live in practical opposition to things as they are. The heirs of the kingdom act in this way upon the world they live in, not by calculation and policy as though they were inspired by another of the world's ideologists, but simply out of the intensity of their sense of the closeness of God and their response to his nature. Their challenge to the world, like that of Jesus himself, must always be an agonized cry, 'How can you do things this way, if God is what he is?'

The early people in William Golding's novel were swept away because they could see only what was there and could not ask 'Why?' But in the New People the power that came from asking 'Why?' turned to destruction because their 'Why?' developed into the whining discontent of a petulant child. Jesus Christ heralds the appearance of an even newer people who have a new question on their lips. They are like St Joan who, in Bernard Shaw's play, says to one of those who cannot understand her: 'You see what is, and you ask, Why? I see what might be, and I ask, Why not?'

27

All This – And Heaven Too

Among the year's autumn books is an expensive anthology, called *I Will See You in Heaven Where Animals Don't Bite*. It has a foreword by Mother Teresa and 74 contributions from such varied authors as Plato and the Dalai Lama, Spike Milligan and George Herbert, Barbara Cartland and Desmond Tutu, all giving their personal views on heaven. For sheer improbable splendour, none can equal Sydney Smith's expectation of eating paté de fois gras to the sound of trumpets. The truth might be that each of us gets what we most want and in due course the eternity of it reveals whether we have chosen heaven or hell.

In the Bible as a whole we can see that belief in a future fulfilment in heaven was a late development. For most of the Old Testament period the Jews believed in something more like Hades, a shadowy afterlife with no vitality and no God. 'Shall thy wonders be known in the dark, and thy righteousness in the land of forgetfulness?' 'For in death there is no remembrance of thee, in the underworld who shall give thee thanks?'

Before dismissing that as a poor and comfortless creed compared with the Christian hope, we would do well to pause and wonder at the vivid, God-centred faith which could sustain the Old Testament prophets without any expectations of heaven. I think we Christians often squander the treasure of our Easter faith self-indulgently, as though the sole significance of Christ's resurrection is that it guarantees our own. We would do better to live the life of this world for God in utter thankfulness, as though it were the only one we have. For unless we learn the delight of living for him here and now unconditionally, I doubt if we shall be capable of much delight hereafter.

In this regard I owe a great deal to a letter I read years ago in one of

Victor Gollancz's books. It was written to him by a fellow undergraduate at Oxford a few days after the outbreak of the First World War, in which he was to lose his life. It ended with this prayer:

> To have given me self-consciousness but for an hour in a world so breathless with beauty would have been enough. But thou hast preserved it within me for twenty years now and more, and hast crowned it with the joy of this summer of summers. And so, come what may, whether life or death, and, if death, whether bliss unimaginable, or nothingness, I thank thee and bless thy name.[1]

If you can, I believe that is the right frame of mind in which to live the Christian life. 'All this!' – and then adding almost as an afterthought – 'and heaven too'.

But for those who are not so fortunate as to see this world 'breathless with beauty', for those who must drag out their days in pain or deprivation or watch a child of theirs being crucified, it makes all the difference when they can say 'and heaven too'. And the New Testament does promise heaven. It promises amendment and restitution, arrival and fulfilment, reward and rest, but it doesn't describe the form that heaven will take. All we are given are elusive images.

From the fourteenth chapter of John's Gospel: 'In my Father's house are many mansions. If it were not so I would have told you, for I go to prepare a place for you.'

From the first letter of John: 'Beloved, even now we are children of God, and it is not yet revealed what we shall be. Yet we know that when it is revealed we shall be like him, for we shall see him even as he is.'

From the twenty-first chapter of Revelation: 'Behold, the tabernacle of God is with men and he shall dwell with them and they shall be his people and God himself shall be with them as their God. And he shall wipe away all tears from their eyes and death shall be no more.'

Beautiful images. But as soon as one asks questions of them they dissolve. And it must be so because we are talking about another dimension of existence which we have never experienced. Here we

[1] *God of a Hundred Names*, compiled by Barbara Greene and Victor Gollancz, Gollancz 1962, p. 222.

are like children developing in the womb of the life to come, children who are not yet ready for birth. Like the human foetus we once were, we cannot imagine any other kind of life. We are secure in the warmth and the dark of our little world. From it we receive our nourishment and are content. Within it we stretch and kick and think we have perfect freedom of movement. We share our mother's life and fancy we know all about relationships. All this time we have been growing lungs without even taking breath, eyes without dreaming what sight means, legs with not a clue about walking. We are equipped for horizons far beyond and do not even know we have the equipment. When the hour of our birth comes we will call it dying because it will be the end of the life we know and we shall be harshly sent out into the unknown. The fact that we cannot imagine heaven does not mean it isn't there and, rather than trying to understand it in advance, we had better get on with the life that is ours now, while our equipment for heaven grows unseen.

There are, however, three clues which I have picked up from three different writers and will briefly pass on to you.

The Roman Catholic philosopher Ladislaus Boros says in his book *The Moment of Truth*[2] that self-abandonment is the one way in which any human person really begins to be. We get a glimpse of this truth whenever we love someone or something completely, but it is at the moment of our birth into the life of heaven, namely what we call the moment of death, that this self-abandonment can be fully realized. 'At that moment', he says,

the individual existence stands, suddenly awake and free, on the frontier of the whole of reality. Being flows towards him like a boundless stream of things, meaning, persons and happenings. Yes, God himself stretches out his hand for him. In a last final decision he either allows this flood of realities to flow past him while he stands there eternally like a rock past which the life-giving stream flows on, or he allows himself to be carried along by this flood, becomes part of it, and flows on into eternal fulfilment.

So entering heaven is joyful self-abandonment to God's life and reality, and this world is the place where we can begin to form the habit.

[2] Burns & Oates 1965.

But that sounds like a rather isolated individual exercise. To counteract that danger I need my second clue, which Austin Farrer gave me in his book *The End of Man*.[3] Like it or not, heaven is other people. Did you think it was God? You are right; but it is God in people, just as it is God in you. 'Then what heaven', exclaims Farrer, 'to be in heaven, and see on every side the glory of God reflected in the image of God which is the human face! What heaven to be in heaven, and to delight, without a barrier, in the company of a thousand friends: when all reserves are down, and all hearts open, and we shall care for the handiwork of God impartially, whether it happens to be in another, or in ourselves!' 'They shall be his people's and God himself shall be with them as their God.'

The last of my three clues as to the nature of heaven comes from St Gregory, the Bishop of Nyssa in the fourth century. For Gregory, heaven is not the end of a journey. In his commentary on the *Song of Songs*, he says that our journey is nothing less than a journey into God and since God is infinite, there can be no journey's end. Through all eternity the road runs on. So there is no boredom in store for us, no holy monotony, but unending adventure and surprise. 'For he that is ascending can always climb higher, and for him who runs towards the Lord the open field of the divine course is never exhausted. We must therefore constantly arouse ourselves and never stop drawing closer and closer in our course.'

'In my Father's estate are many stopping-places. See, I am going ahead to prepare a place for you.'

---

[3] SPCK 1973.

28

An Easter People

All authority in heaven and on earth has been given to me. Go therefore and make disciples of all nations, baptizing them in the name of the Father and of the Son and of the Holy Spirit, and teaching them to obey all that I have commanded you. And remember, I am with you always. (Matthew 28.18–20)

The end of Matthew's Gospel is set, not in Jerusalem, as in Luke's Gospel, but in Galilee. There is an important difference. Jerusalem is the stronghold of traditional faith and orthodox worship, everything that most of us mean by 'the church'. The Risen Christ does indeed meet us there in prayer and sacrament, fellowship and festival. But the Lord intends us to experience the fullness of Easter outside the routine life of the church. Galilee is the world of work, the commercial arena, the centre of radical politics. When the living Christ meets us there we can be sure that something utterly new has happened, and resurrection is not just an item in the creed but a startling fact of experience.

The closing words of that Gospel contain the four 'all's – the complete and universal range of the claims of the Risen Christ. *All authority* in heaven and on earth tells us that his claims are not restricted to the spiritual sphere but encompass the whole earthly realm of business and nationhood, society and politics. *All nations* are equally the scene in which we can expect to find disciples; so human response to Jesus Christ is not restricted to one culture or history or religion. *All the commands* which Christ himself has given are to be laid upon us and all other disciples; so we are not free to pick and choose, nor to mould his kingdom to suit our preferences. *All the days* are going to be transformed by his abiding presence. In the bad days as well as the good ones, in all periods of history, in all our varying moods, we may know Emmanuel, God with us.

The supreme responsibility of the Christian is to bear witness to

the resurrection of Jesus Christ. When the apostles were looking for
someone to fill the gap made by the defection and suicide of poor
Judas Iscariot, they looked for someone who could 'become with us a
witness to his resurrection'. That is the true basis and the true meaning of
anything we can call 'the apostolic tradition'. It is to enter into the
apostles' experience of the resurrection in order to join in the apostles'
proclamation of the resurrection. That is the inheritance and the task
which we are asked to take into our weak human hands – 'With us to
become a witness to his resurrection'.

Those apostles had passed through the deepest despair and the
most unbearable sense of guilt that any people have suffered.

During all that time when Jesus was going in and out among them
they had seen how perfectly he had lived out his vision of love and
truth, and with what childlike trust he had relied on God. If his
terrible cry of betrayal from the cross was really the last word and all
the rest was silence, then this world has neither justice nor meaning.
But to the hopelessness and anger and loss of faith in those apostles
was added an appalling burden of shame. They had abandoned their
leader in cowardice. When God lets you down you can ease your pain
with rage, but when it is you who have let God down there is no
alleviation.

No one who has fallen so deep in bitterness and guilt can recover
confidence or a sense of direction without years of struggle. Yet
within a few days those apostles were more certain, more radiantly
committed than they had ever been before. Nothing could have lifted
them from such a depth to such a height except an overwhelming
encounter with all that they thought they had lost. They knew God
was to be trusted because the one thing that could reverse the tragedy
of Jesus's crucifixion and heaven's dreadful silence had happened.
They knew they were forgiven because they had met the one person
who could forgive them whom they had never expected to see again.
It was as though they themselves had died and come to life again. The
resurrection of Jesus had given them a kind of resurrection of their
own.

And that is the evidence of Easter even today. When people see
those who have been lifted out of a wreckage of disillusionment and
guilt into a sure and certain hope, not by a slow and partial recovery
but in a sudden release that may not necessarily come in religious
terms at all, then they cannot deny that some glorious Lord of life is at
work. They take knowledge of them that they have been with Jesus.

When Pope John Paul II spoke in North America he said, 'We are the Easter people and our song is Alleluia.' Never forget that you are an Easter people called to become witnesses of his resurrection. When you bring children or adults for baptism into the dying and rising of Christ, and when you partake in bread and wine of the presence of one who has died and is alive for evermore, remember that you are accepting for your own affairs and decisions in the world the eternal pattern of life through death, constantly laying life down, letting something go, in the faith that fuller, richer life will follow for yourself or for someone else. When you are trying to help others in perplexity or trouble, especially the young or the parents of the young, remember that you are on the side of life and that God is more concerned that his children should be fully alive than that they should be religious.

So in our church life we must build up the religion that makes people more aware and sensitive and brings them to life, but set our face as Jesus did against the religion that deadens the hearts and the minds of people. When we share in the church's concern for human society as spokespersons for the kingdom of God's righteousness, we must remember that we are the messengers of hopefulness. In a world of sceptical manipulation we must keep on affirming that human nature *can* be changed, and that the future of our nation and our world is not being made by *us* nor marred by *us* but is coming to meet us from the hand of God. And, when we meet to discuss the maintenance and mission of our local church we need to remember that the tradition of which we are the guardians is not a village pond of stagnant water but a bubbling spring of newness of life, a new wine that will always break the old wineskins generation after generation, and that we are guardians of the wine, not the skins. The church remains true to its past by moving forward because it is the servant of him who says, 'Behold, I am making all things new.'

But no one can become a witness to the resurrection simply by attending to outward acts and attitudes. Just as the Easter fire can be lit only from the Paschal candle, so a convincing witness to the resurrection can be generated only from contact with the Risen Christ himself. Serious Christians must take time in whatever way has the greatest reality for them to keep up that never-ending pursuit of yearning, grateful love which Paul described in the third chapter of his letter to the Philippians:

I want to know Christ and the power of his resurrection and the sharing of his sufferings by becoming like him in his death, if somehow I may attain the resurrection from the dead. Not that I have already obtained this or have already reached the goal; but I press on to make it my own because Christ Jesus has made me his own.

29

The Winds of the Spirit

In my first curacy in central London I was asked to take charge of a children's church on Sunday afternoons. One Whit Sunday we were talking about the wind. Had anyone ever seen the wind? No ... but yes, you could see that it was a windy day even by looking through the window. How could you tell? Clouds racing across the sky, trees bending and tossing, a man running down the street after his hat. Then the children settled down in twos and threes to draw pictures of the wind. Five minutes later I was given a handful of designs that would have helped any of us to understand why, on that Pentecost morning in Jerusalem when the Holy Spirit first came upon the church, the whole house was suddenly filled with the sound of a rushing mighty wind.

Two of the children, a brother and sister, must have had parents who could afford a yacht, because they had drawn and coloured a really expert picture of a boat leaning before the wind, its sails filled and spray rising high around the prow. There was the powerful Spirit of life, the onward drive of God's good purpose that we might have life and have it to the full. We are asked only to spread our sails and trust ourselves wholly to his will and direction. We cannot plot the course in advance nor know our destination, for the wind blows where it will and we have no idea whence it comes or whither it is going. So is everyone that is born of the Spirit.

The saints have always known that the secret of life is to trust the unseen and run before the wind. St Columba's great mission to the North, which changed the face of Scotland and of Northumbria for the next two centuries, began when he set out from Ulster with twelve companions in his boat and let the wind and the tides carry them wherever it might be. Because it was a penance for the dreadful slaughter in a tribal battle that Columba considered his own wilfulness had brought about, they could not settle where they first struck land because the mountains of Mourne were still visible far, far off across the sea. So once again they trusted themselves to the wind, and this time it brought them to Iona.

The apostle Paul travelled in the same way too on his mission. Having been prevented by the Holy Spirit from preaching in the province of Asia, he and his companions travelled through Phrygia and Galatia, and when they tried to enter Bithynia, the Spirit of Jesus would not allow them. So they skirted Mysia and reached the coast at Troas. And while they stayed in that small grubby port, Paul had the vision that directed him across the channel into Europe.

Such is the freedom, the spontaneity, the uninhibited response to circumstance which we see in Jesus of Nazareth. It is indeed his Spirit, and it can make us as vividly alive as he also was, his free Spirit, the Spirit of true aliveness.

Another picture that those children produced for me showed a tree bending before a gale, with autumn leaves streaming away from the stretched branches. In our prayers, we ask that the Holy Spirit will renew the face of the land. We know that he is the Spirit of life, of perpetual springtime; but there can be no spring until there has been the stripping of autumn and winter. New shoots, new leaves, can never grow on the beech tree until those dry, beautiful leaves of autumn which cling so tightly all through the winter, are finally stripped away. For the old must go before the new can come. That is part of the very way and principle of life. And the Holy Spirit is intent on a continual stripping away of that which has served its purpose and should be allowed to go in order that renewal may come.

There are many, many ideas which have been true and have served us in their day, but they become outdated, outmoded, the language is wrong, the general direction of the idea is somehow no longer inspiring. We must be prepared to let things go. If we cling too tenaciously to what we choose to call 'principle', we may lose that very life and spontaneity that the Spirit would give us. Of course it is painful, but the Spirit of truth is constantly in the business of renewing our perception of truth, cleansing our vision, so that we may move forward with God and be still of service to his ever-renewed world.

The Spirit of truth acts by posing questions. He questions our presumptions, our assumptions, our certainties. The church seems always to be terrified of questions. There is always a row whenever something that seems established is questioned. And so it is difficult to recognize very often that this is the Spirit of truth who is at work. He will not deceive us, he will not lead us into falsehood, he will preserve that which is eternally true – but he will do it by constantly cleansing our vision so that we see it afresh. But if we insist on the old words, the old terminology, the old way of phrasing things, and believe that our life consists in what has been, we shall miss the many-splendoured thing and actually deviate from the eternal truth. The Bible is full of those Spirit-filled questions, the ancient questions of integrity. Where art thou? Where is your brother? What are you doing here, Elijah? What are you looking for, Andrew? Do you say this of yourself, or did some other tell it to you? And when those awkward questions arise in our minds, we must not close our ears, for it is the Spirit, the life-giver, who stirs this questioning within us, insists that we look again at what we take for granted, because there is a springtime of the mind that still awaits us, however old and settled we may have become. Let the old leaves be stripped away by the questioning Spirit of truth so that that springtime may be restored to us.

A third picture was of a windmill. It looked very static. There was in fact in the picture no sign of movement, nothing to show the sails revolving, because everything was going on *inside*. That is where the wheels were turning and the great stones grinding. And this is another very important gift of the Holy Spirit. Perhaps it has special significance for those of us who have passed the main years of violent activity, who are perhaps unwillingly reduced to sitting still for quite a lot of the time, apparently static. But if the Spirit is with you, there will be a great milling going on inside. For now the harvest has been reaped, the experiences have mostly been lived through. What will you make of them? As you sit and ponder all that you have seen and known, if the Holy Spirit is with you there will be bread, not just for you but for many, many others.

The Spirit is the Spirit of contemplation. Quietly he enables you to understand what has been. In his life and in his truth he unfolds the significance of what has happened and you see the richness of it, and your heart warms and love is born – love that stretches beyond your ordinary affections, your ordinary associations. Love for life, love for the world, love for little things, love for people that you have never met is actually brought to birth as you meditate on what you have known and experienced. It is the bread of our love that is produced by this quiet milling over, which is also the work of the Holy Spirit. 'He will bring to mind', says Jesus, 'all that I have told you.' You will go over it and realize how much the Lord has given, how much the Lord has revealed, but there is still much more to be revealed, and as you see it your heart will deepen with a greater love.

These then are the gifts of the Spirit, the Spirit of life, the Spirit of truth, the Spirit of love – all that rushing, mighty wind that will always and for ever have us in its grasp.

30

Being Alive

All of us have suffered from the man – it almost always is a man – who feels his call is to be the life and soul of the party. His relentless jocularity soon has everybody looking away in bored embarrassment. The reason? Because he is so arrogantly self-appointed, so self-conscious in what he is doing.

The true life-giver is quite different. Some years ago an article appeared in *The Tablet* written by an American woman who had made it her business to improve the general lifestyle of a large number of old people's homes. She described how she went into one such home in New York where it was customary to find the inmates, as one might horribly call them, sitting in a circle around the edge of the large room, almost half-dead, she said; nobody talking to anyone. Everybody frozen, still, waiting, endlessly waiting.

She was determined to make a change; and one day she invited a young dancer to visit them. As the music played on the record-player and the girl danced in the centre of the room, little by little the old people began to sway and to move and to strike the time with their hands. They were caught up in *her* life. One man was seen to stare at his hand and heard to exclaim: 'My God, it is ten years since I moved that hand!' And a 104-year-old German lady was heard to mutter: 'It reminds me of when I danced for the Tsar of Russia!'

Life-giving is contagious. Life itself, real aliveness as in that young dancer, is catching. And that is what lies behind the story from the seventh chapter of Luke's Gospel of the raising to life again of the man who was the only son of his widowed mother.

It first of all strikes us, I think, as a little odd, a little tame, that when this greatest of all miracles was performed by Jesus and he actually raised the dead, the people round about him said, 'A great prophet has arisen in our midst.' Is that all? Just another prophet? But, you see, Nain, where the story is set, is only two or three miles from another village called Shunem which is where the prophet Elisha had raised from death the young son whom through prayer he had brought to a childless woman. The story is told in chapter 4 of the second book of Kings. And that healing miracle by Elisha has extraordinary similarities to the story of Elijah, an earlier prophet, told in the first book of Kings, chapter 17.

The prophet is essentially alive. He is alive to God, more aware of the reality of God and of God's force and designs than most of us. He is alive to the world around him. He sees the great movements of politics, the morality or lack of it that lies within a society. He is aware of every aspect of the world: its tragedy, its beauty, its glory and promise. And he is alive towards other people. He knows what they are thinking. He can tell them what is going on within them.

That fellow-feeling is the hallmark of the prophet. In both instances of raising the dead, the prophet 'cramped himself' (that's the true translation – not 'stretched'). He made himself the size of the little boy, putting, in Elisha's case, his eyes on the child's eyes and his mouth on the child's mouth and his hands on the little child's hands. His self-identification, making himself one with the weak and the needy and the small; coming down to our level. That godlike smallness is the mark of the aliveness of the prophet who must feel our infirmities, our weakness, while at the same time the prophet has the life that is contagious. In both cases that statement is true.

Immediately Elijah put the child on his own bed. There was a nearness, a personal contact, in that action. In the woman of Shunem's case she immediately takes the child into the little room that was the prophet's and lays him on the prophet's bed, not on hers, in order that he might without delay be in contact with Elisha's greater reserves of life.

That is the true 'life and soul of the party'. It happened in the case of the dancer. Her aliveness became contagious. Aliveness always is. This is more true of that greatest prophet, Jesus of Nazareth, than of any other human being. He was essentially alive, in the very depth alive; alive to God, alive to the world and alive to each human being in his inwardness. He was so alive, that it is from him that we take our life.

Again and again we end our prayers with those words, 'our Lord Jesus Christ *who is alive* and reigns with God the Father and the Holy Spirit'. 'Who is alive' – that essential virtue of the Lord Jesus Christ whereby we come alive. 'Because I am alive', he says, 'you shall come alive also.' That is why he gives us the sacrament; because it is a sacrament of touch, of contact, of taking the life from him and making it our own.

31

The Fruit of the Spirit

But the fruit of the Spirit is love, joy, peace, long-suffering, kindness, goodness, faith, meekness and self-control. (Galatians 5.22–3)

The trouble is that we Christians so often imagine that we are Christmas trees. We strive to make our rather bare, dry characters more attractive by acquiring these virtues one by one and displaying them like silver stars or coloured balls hung from our branches as gorgeous fruits. We are ready to pay quite a high price to get hold of them, especially the bigger, high-sounding sort at the top of the list. Love, joy, peace – we like to talk about them. Meekness and self-control are not so interesting. They lack sparkle.

But human personalities are not Christmas trees. They are more like the trees of the forest. They vary from one another and each one is all of a piece, bearing its own kind of fruit and no other, although it may be good or bad of its kind, and that is what matters. So what Paul is giving to the Galatians in this well-known passage isn't a spiritual shopping list for some kind of greengrocer or fruiterer of virtues, but a portrait, a character-sketch of a single integrated personality.

Does this seem to conflict with Paul's use of the phrase 'the fruit of the Spirit'? Is it natural to speak of a human personality as fruit? It was, for the writers of the Old and New Testaments who were more conscious than we are that we always have used the same words for bearing a crop and bearing a child, bringing forth fruit or bringing forth a baby. We do use the same language, there is a connection, a likeness. In the Bible the ideas of birth and harvest are never far apart. So the fruit of the Spirit, which Paul contrasts with the works of the flesh, is really very similar to 'that which is born of the Spirit' whom Jesus in the Gospel of John contrasts with 'that which is born of the flesh'.

So far from there being a shopping-list of virtues, what Paul is presenting to the Christians of Galatia is a portrait of the person whom the Holy Spirit brings to birth.

Who is that? Who is born when anyone is born again? Christ. Who else but Jesus is Paul describing in these two verses? For these verses are just one of the two portraits which he has painted for us, extraordinarily true to the figure that we meet in the Gospels. There is no doubt who is in his mind when he gives us this list of characteristics. So let's read it beginning from the end, with those less popular qualities:

Self-control means being in power, having mastery. The Greek word is *encrateia*, literally, 'being in power', and it belongs to the same family as democrat – people power; plutocrat – wealth power; bureaucrat – committee power; theocracy – being in God's power, having God's power. That is what Jesus had when, after his temptations, 'he returned in the power of the Spirit' to start his ministry.

Meekness is a quality Jesus attributed to himself when he said: 'I am meek and of a humble heart.' I don't throw my weight around, I don't take a tough line.

Faith means faithful trustworthiness. It also means trustfulness. It is the very opposite of being suspicious of people, trusting even those who don't deserve trust.

Goodness means benevolence and generosity. It is the goodness to which Jesus refers at the end of the parable of the vineyard owner and those waiting to be employed. When the master gives the same wages to all of them, and the others who had worked longer begin to grumble, he says, 'Is your eye evil envious because I am good [generous]?'

Gentleness is really a word which in our modern jargon means 'user-friendly'. 'My yoke is easy', he said, and it is the same word as this gentleness. It is smooth, it fits, it doesn't rub, it isn't harsh.

Long-suffering is patience, endurance. This came to Jesus's mouth when he said, 'How long' must I bear with you, how long must I suffer your lack of faith? But I must, because I am patient.

Peace is that tranquillity shown by Jesus when under pressure, in the face of disappointments, and when he lay calmly asleep in the boat during the storm. He says, 'Peace is my parting gift to you, *my* peace I give to you. Not as the world gives, give I to you.'

Joy is something else he gives to his followers: 'I have said these things to you that my joy might be in you and your joy become complete.'

Love brings us to the second of these portraits that Paul has written with Jesus in mind, the famous passage in the thirteenth chapter of his first letter to the Corinthians, where we almost have the same character revealed, the same list. Patiently enduring is love; it is gentle, like the easy yoke and the smooth wine; it is not envious, but generous like that master in the parable, generous-hearted; never boastful or conceited or rude, but humble, unselfish, meek; not quick-tempered, doesn't keep score of wrongs or take pleasure in other people's sins; on the contrary, love delights in truth, and puts up with every disappointment, always trustful, hopeful, holding on, never giving up.

What Paul is giving us in both passages is a portrait of Jesus himself, because the fruit of the Spirit is nothing less than the life of the living Christ brought to birth within the Christian fellowship as a whole and within the individual disciple. That is what happened at Pentecost. In fact, Paul says as much in very clear terms elsewhere in this same letter to the Galatians. In chapter 2, at the end of a long autobiographical section, he declares: 'The life I now live is not my life, but the life which Christ lives in me.' Then in chapter 4 he says, 'You are my own children and I am in labour with you all over again until' – Paul does not say 'until you are born again', he says – 'until Christ is formed in you.' That is something totally different from trying to adorn our lives in God's sight by attaching a little more love, a little more self-control. Instead it is letting Christ live out within us his own unique relationship with his Father. So Paul says again in this same letter: 'To ensure that you are his children, God has sent into our hearts the Spirit, the Breath, of his Son, crying his special name, Abba, Father!' Jesus praying in us, moment by moment, Father, here I am.

This is the meaning of the sacramental action of the Risen Christ recorded in the Gospel reading for Pentecost, from John's Gospel, chapter 20: 'Peace be with you. As the Father sent me, so I am sending you.' After saying this, he breathed on them and said, 'Receive the Holy Spirit.' The breath, the life, of Jesus himself. It was what he had promised in that upper room just three nights earlier. 'I will not leave you as orphans. I will come to you. When that day comes you will know that I am in my Father and you in me, and I in you ... Those who dwell in me as I dwell in them, bear much fruit.'

Many years ago there was in the Church of South India a simple catechist who previously had worked as a carpenter. He was put in charge of a group of little churches, but because he was such a simple man, he muddled up the accounts of the collections from those churches, was rather harshly judged as having possibly played fast and loose with church money and was dismissed from his post. Covered in shame, he moved right away from that area and disappeared. He went to a very remote tribal area up in the hills. It was not until many years afterwards that people from the churches sent forth their evangelists and missionaries into that area, where they began very simply to tell the story of Jesus Christ. And to their astonishment, they were met by the villagers who were listening to them with the words, 'Oh, we know who you are talking about, but he didn't die as you say. He came and lived with us. He only died three or four years ago. We didn't know that his name was Jesus, because he didn't tell us what he was called. We only knew him simply as the carpenter.'

32

Doing and Being

Trinity Sunday and all those Sundays after Trinity are a very English
and a very Anglican institution. Now there is a move to bring the
Anglican Church into line with with more ancient use and to name
the second half of the Christian year the Sundays after Pentecost. The
idea appeals to me because we need reminding that the Holy Spirit is
the one, never-failing source of life and love to the church. And yet,
for another reason, I would be sad to lose our peculiarly accidental
attachment to the Holy Trinity. I wonder whether you have come
across these verses written by J. M. Falkner early in this century?

> We have done with dogma and divinity,
> Easter and Whitsun past,
> The long, long Sundays after Trinity
> Are with us at last;
> The passionless Sundays after Trinity,
> Neither feast day nor fast.
>
> Christmas comes with plenty,
> Lent spreads out its pall,
> But these are five and twenty,
> The longest Sundays of all;
> The placid Sundays after Trinity,
> Wheat harvest, fruit harvest, Fall.

And that, surely, is the true rhythm and the natural division of our
annual cycle. Half a year to tell and retell the events of our salvation;
half a year to work that salvation deeper into our daily living. Six
months to celebrate what God has done; six months to contemplate
what God is. Doing and Being.

What you are weighs more than what you do. If there is a

judgement, either at the end of time, or at the crisis moments during time, it is what you are in yourself that is judged, more than what you have done. If a child or an animal gives you its trust or its love, it is not for the things you have done, but because it has an instinct for what manner of person you are.

Yet you can only be what you are prepared to do. No one is brave until he has committed himself to an act of courage. No one is honest unless her truth is put to the test. There is no love without one being given to another.

And so it is with God. The philosophers speak of pure Being, but I take leave to doubt if they know what they are talking about. God is love because God is committed to loving. What God did in Christ, in the long Advent preparation of his people, through the coming at Bethlehem to the cross at Jerusalem, and on to the ascent of the Risen Lord and the descent of the Spirit, was the inevitable outworking of what God is, the shining glory of the Invisible. By reflecting upon these events we learn to understand what kind of God God is. We see he is a God eternally committed to identifying himself with what he loves. Eternally committed to the pattern of death and resurrection, letting go for the sake of fuller life. God is a cruciform reality. But it is just as true to say that that series of events from Christmas to Easter was what God had to be eternally committed to *do* in order to *be* the almighty and most merciful Father to all people at all times.

The events we celebrate from Advent to Pentecost not only reveal but confirm the divine nature that we contemplate on Trinity Sunday and the Sundays after.

The doctrine of a God whose Being can be known as Three in One may have been devised as a way of explaining how Jesus Christ could be the eternal Son and Word and Image of God. But it has so enriched our understanding of God's nature, and of our own nature also, that even if the church were to find some other, equally adequate way of expressing the truth of Jesus Christ we could never again do without this idea of a Trinity in Unity.

Think of it in relation to God's eternal Being, the I AM of God.

God is what he is.
God knows what he is.
God knows the worth of what he is.

God being what he is we call the Father.

God knowing what he is we call the Son, God's image of himself, God's name for himself.

God knowing the worth of what he is, not self-esteem but simple acceptance of the value of being what he is, we call the Spirit.

And immediately, don't you see, we have gained a profound insight into our own being, we see what it means truly to say, I am. It means being myself as I am, not as I am dressed up, and being myself all through. It means knowing what I am, without fantasies or false images of myself, either as an angel or a devil. And it means knowing the worth of that self, accepting and loving that self without pride or hatred because it is unique, and because I am, in fact, already loved. It is so simple and yet the hardest task in the world, to say 'I am' with that kind of maturity, modelled on God's I AM. But Jesus said 'Be complete as your heavenly Father is complete.'

Or think of this Trinity in Unity in terms of the two activities we associate supremely with God – that he loves and that he creates.

God is love – not static but dynamic energy of love, all aspects of love. In him is the love that initiates the loving. In him also is the love that receives and responds – never forget that. The initiating love we call the Father: the responsive love we call the Son. But in him also is the awareness of that flow of love between one and the other which sees and values its infinite worth and bliss. This loving awareness and evaluation we call the Holy Spirit. Yet all is one complete love.

And doesn't that tell us immediately the true pattern of all love, all deep relationship? Many marriages are starved, many families frustrated, because one person assumes that he or she must do all the loving and has never learned how to receive love, how to allow the marriage partner or the child to initiate love from their side sometimes. Or again, we love so compulsively, out of such need, that we never stand back from the relationship to see it truly and evaluate it with humility and joy. So it always has to be said of us that we know not what we do.

Again, God is Creator. And in the energy of creation we see the same Trinity. There is the initiating idea, the dream, the plan, of something that never was. God dreamed this universe before he made it. God imagined and loved you before time began. Then, in response to the initiating idea, there is the effort to give the idea form and actuality. And again, at the same time, there is the creative awareness that evaluates the force of the idea and the effectiveness of the form it is given, and sees that it is good, or less than good. Planning and performance and evaluation: Father, Son and Holy Spirit. Yet all is a single act of creation.

Once more we see that this is the essential structure of all creativity and all work. Every work of art or music is a unity consisting of the idea, the form and the critical appreciation. Here, too, we have the simple theological reason why the behavioural scientists tell us that job satisfaction can be found only when the work is so organized and distributed that every worker enjoys some real share in the planning, the performance and the evaluation of a complete task in the work process. This is true of the industrial plant and of the municipal office. And the redemption of our complex technical society is to be found in remodelling our institutions on the pattern of the nature of God, the Holy Trinity.

That should not surprise us, nor sound so quaintly obscure. For if this is God's world then his stamp is upon every particle of it, his name on every product, his own inner nature reproduced in the way everything works

To know what he is like, what manner of God he is, we look again and again at the story of the Man of Bethlehem and Galilee and Calvary. And, having renewed that image and pattern in our minds, we reflect upon the wonder of a God who can be like that in all his dealings with us, who has committed himself to that for us. And we try to model our own selves, our family loves, our institutions, our cities, and the kingdoms of this world upon the pattern of the nature of this God. To do this is the merest common sense for each one of us, for it is no more than acknowledging the reality we must live with. This is our truest worship and our most reasonable service, and all the Sundays after Trinity will not be time enough for it.

Sources

The poem which appears at the beginning of Part One, called 'Easter', was included in *A Christmas Sequence and Other Poems*, published in 1989 by The Amate Press. At the beginning of Part Two is the last verse of a poem called 'Avignon'.

The sermons were preached on the following occasions:

1 In the End Is the Beginning
    Advent Sunday, 29 November 1992
2 In the Beginning Was the Word
    Second Sunday after Christmas, 9 January 1994
3 The Moment in Time
    Watch-night services, 31 December 1990 and 1992
4 The Shining Appearance
    Epiphany, 6 January 1991
5 From Revelation to Revolution
    Epiphany, 5 January 1986
6 The Wine Poured Forth
    Fifth Sunday in Lent, 28 March 1993
7 God Was in Christ
    Talk given at Christ Church, Bath, 6 February 1994
8 And God Raised Him Up
    Winchester Cathedral, Easter Day 1977 or 1978
9 The Easter God
    Sunday after Easter, 19 April 1998
10 The Self-Giving God
    All Saints' Convent Chapel, Pentecost, 30 May 1993
11 The Nature of God
    Chapel of Trinity College, Cambridge, Trinity Sunday, 2 June 1996

Index